MacBook Air 2025 M4 Chip User Guide

Master New Features, Boost Performance, and Optimize Your Workflow with Step-by-Step Instructions

Oksana Chalifour

Table Of Contents

INTRODUCTION

Apple's **MacBook Air (M4, 2025)** is a marvel of modern technology, bringing together the perfect blend of **power**, **portability**, and **efficiency** in a lightweight, eco-friendly design. Whether you're a student, business professional, creator, or even a casual gamer, the MacBook Air (M4, 2025) is engineered to elevate your computing experience. Apple has refined and redefined what a thin and light laptop can do, and this model is an exceptional testament to that innovation.

In this review, we'll break down everything about the **MacBook Air (M4, 2025)** in a **step-by-step** guide, covering its design, the power of the **M4 chip**, its performance across different use cases, and how it compares to other models within Apple's lineup.

Key Features and Overview

- **Lightweight and Thin Design**: Weighing only **2.8 pounds** and measuring just **0.63 inches thick**, it remains one of the most portable laptops available.

- **Stunning Retina Display**: The **13.6-inch Liquid Retina display** boasts **500 nits of brightness**, **True Tone**, and **P3 wide color**, making it perfect for everything from creative work to entertainment.

- **Exceptional Battery Life**: With **up to 18 hours** of video playback and **15 hours** of web browsing, it's perfect for long days at school, work, or travel.

- **Eco-friendly Build**: Apple continues its commitment to sustainability by using **100% recycled aluminum** in the chassis, making it a **carbon-neutral** device.

Introduction to the M4 Chip and Its Role in Performance

At the heart of the **MacBook Air (M4, 2025)** is Apple's cutting-edge **M4 chip**, which brings unparalleled performance and efficiency improvements.

Key aspects of the **M4 chip**:

- **8-Core CPU**: With 8 high-performance cores, the M4 chip is significantly faster and more energy-efficient than previous models, offering up to **60% better performance** compared to the M1 chip.

- **10-Core GPU**: The M4's GPU boosts graphics performance, making it suitable for light gaming, **photo editing**, and **video rendering**.

- **16-Core Neural Engine**: This allows for smarter, AI-driven experiences, enhancing tasks like **image recognition**, **speech recognition**, and **advanced creative workflows**.

The **M4 chip** ensures the MacBook Air can handle everything from everyday tasks to more demanding applications, all while maintaining impressive battery efficiency.

Who Should Buy the MacBook Air?

The **MacBook Air (M4, 2025)** is versatile enough to cater to a wide variety of users:

- **Beginners**: With its easy-to-use **macOS** interface and seamless integration with Apple's ecosystem, the MacBook Air is perfect for new users. The **lightweight design** and **long battery life** make it ideal for students or anyone looking for an accessible entry into the world of Apple.

- **Business Professionals**: For professionals who need a **reliable** and **portable** device, the MacBook Air offers **excellent performance**, **strong security features** (like **Touch ID**), and an exceptional **battery life** for long meetings or travel.

- **Gamers**: While not designed specifically for **high-end gaming**, the MacBook Air (M4) can handle casual gaming and cloud gaming platforms like **Apple Arcade** and **GeForce Now** thanks to its **10-core GPU**.

- **Creators**: Whether you're into **photo editing**, **video production**, or **graphic design**, the MacBook Air's enhanced GPU and **Neural Engine** are ideal for **creative workflows**.

Why Choose the MacBook Air Over Other Models?

- **MacBook Pro Comparison**: If you're someone who needs more ports, **advanced GPU** performance, and a larger display, the **MacBook Pro** would be a better fit. However, for users who prioritize **portability**, **long battery life**, and a **lightweight design**, the **MacBook Air (M4, 2025)** delivers fantastic value without the bulk of the Pro model.

- **MacBook Air vs. Older Models**: The **M4 chip** delivers significantly improved **graphics performance** and **battery life** compared to the **M1**, **M2**, and **M3** chips. It also brings **AI integration** to the table, allowing for faster processing and smarter features across macOS and apps.

What's New in the 2025 MacBook Air Model?

M4 Chip vs. M1, M2, and M3 Chips: What's the Difference?

Here's a breakdown of how the **M4 chip** compares to its predecessors:

- **M1 Chip**: The **M1** was a game-changer in terms of efficiency and performance. However, the **M4 chip** improves on the **M1** by offering a better **GPU**, more power-efficient **AI processing**, and **longer battery life**.

- **M2 Chip**: While the **M2** offered a performance upgrade over the **M1**, the **M4** chip surpasses it with **enhanced graphics**, **better AI integration**, and a stronger overall performance boost.

- **M3 Chip**: The **M3** was a solid improvement but still lacked the **AI advancements** and **efficiency** of the **M4 chip**.

The **M4 chip** is a clear leap forward, providing users with not just **more speed** but **smarter performance** and more **efficient power usage**.

AI Integration and How It Enhances User Experience

The **M4 chip** features a **16-core Neural Engine**, designed to handle AI-powered tasks like:

- **Image Processing**: Applications like **Adobe Photoshop** can process images faster with **AI-enhanced tools**.

- **Voice and Speech Recognition**: Apps like **Siri** and voice-to-text capabilities become more **accurate** and **responsive**.

- **Smart Task Management**: The **AI system** helps manage system resources, making sure apps run smoothly without wasting energy or causing slowdowns.

These **AI capabilities** make the MacBook Air (M4) feel faster, smarter, and more intuitive, creating a smoother experience overall.

New Battery Life Improvements and Performance

With the **M4 chip**'s efficiency, the MacBook Air (M4, 2025) achieves exceptional battery performance:

- **Up to 18 hours** of video playback.

- **Up to 15 hours** of web browsing.

This is a significant improvement, giving you the freedom to work, study, or play all day without worrying about recharging.

Advanced Graphics and Display Technologies

The **M4 chip's 10-core GPU** offers an impressive boost in graphics performance. Whether you're:

- **Photo editing** in **Lightroom** or **Photoshop**.

- **Editing videos** in **Final Cut Pro**.

- **Playing games** on **Apple Arcade**.

The **M4 chip** ensures smooth, high-quality graphics with no lag, all displayed beautifully on the **13.6-inch Liquid Retina** screen, which offers vibrant colors and sharp clarity.

Setting Expectations for the MacBook Air

What Are the Key Strengths of the MacBook Air?

The MacBook Air (M4, 2025) offers several standout features:

- **Portability**: At just **2.8 pounds** and **0.63 inches thick**, it's one of the most portable laptops on the market.

- **Performance**: The **M4 chip** delivers top-tier performance for daily tasks, **light creative work**, and **casual gaming**.

- **Battery Life**: With **up to 18 hours** of video playback, it will last through even the busiest days without needing to recharge.

- **Eco-friendly**: Made from **100% recycled aluminum**, it's a **carbon-neutral** device, contributing to a more sustainable future.

What Are the Potential Limitations?

Despite its impressive features, there are a few limitations:

- **Limited Ports**: The MacBook Air only has **two Thunderbolt 3 ports** and a **MagSafe charging port**, which could be limiting for users who require more **USB-A ports**, **SD card slots**, or **HDMI** connections. However, external adapters or docking stations can help resolve this.

- **No Dedicated GPU**: While the **M4's 10-core GPU** is great for everyday graphics tasks, it might struggle with **intensive gaming** or **high-end video rendering**. For those needs, the **MacBook Pro** models with **dedicated GPUs** are more suitable.

Ideal Use Cases for Different Users

- **Business Professionals**: With **powerful performance**, a **long-lasting battery**, and seamless integration with other Apple products, the MacBook Air is perfect for professionals who need a reliable, secure, and lightweight laptop for daily business tasks.

- **Gamers**: While not specifically built for **high-end gaming**, it's capable of **casual gaming** and cloud gaming, making it ideal for users who want to enjoy games via services like **Apple Arcade** and **GeForce Now**.

- **Creative Professionals**: For **photo editing**, **video production**, and **graphic design**, the MacBook Air offers excellent performance, especially with the **M4 chip**'s improved **GPU** and **AI-enhanced capabilities**.

The **MacBook Air (M4, 2025)** is an incredibly versatile device that caters to a variety of users. Its **portability**, **performance**, and **long battery life** make it an ideal choice for anyone—from beginners to professionals, gamers to creators. Whether you're looking for a laptop to carry to class, work on business projects, edit videos, or simply enjoy some light gaming, the MacBook Air (M4, 2025) is more than up to the task.

DESIGN AND BUILD QUALITY

The **MacBook Air (M4, 2025)** brings a stunning balance of form, function, and sustainability. In this section, we'll walk you through the design, build quality, display, keyboard, trackpad, and charging ports, explaining how to get the best results from each feature.

Ultra-Light, Thin, and Durable Aluminum Unibody

The MacBook Air's **unibody aluminum** construction is designed to be lightweight yet **exceptionally strong**. The **machined aluminum** gives it a **premium feel** while ensuring durability. It is incredibly **thin**, making it an excellent choice for those who need portability without sacrificing strength. The use of **recycled aluminum** also makes it an eco-friendly option for consumers conscious about sustainability.

How to Maximize Durability and Portability:

1. **Handling with Care**:

    o While the MacBook Air is built to be **lightweight and portable**, it's also very **sleek**. When carrying your MacBook, make sure to use a **protective sleeve** or **case** to prevent scratches or scuff marks, especially on the edges of the aluminum.

o   For additional protection, **avoid placing sharp objects** (like pens or keys) directly inside your bag with the MacBook.

2. **Optimal Usage:**

    o   If you're **traveling frequently** or commuting, the MacBook Air's ultra-thin design will fit into most bags or backpacks with ease. Its **light weight (2.8 pounds)** means you can carry it comfortably without feeling burdened.

    o   When setting the MacBook down, be cautious about **placing it on rough surfaces** to avoid any scratches on the aluminum.

Sustainability Advantage:

- The aluminum unibody is made from **100% recycled materials**, contributing to a smaller carbon footprint. This means your MacBook is both a high-performance device and an eco-conscious choice for the environmentally aware.

Available Colors and Customization Options

Color Options Available: The MacBook Air (M4, 2025) offers four stunning color choices to match your style:

1. **Space Gray** – A professional, sleek, and classic look.

2. **Silver** – Bright and timeless, offering a polished and refined aesthetic.

3. **Starlight** – A soft, warm gold with a refined finish.

4. **Midnight** – A rich, deep blue that stands out in a subtle yet stylish way.

How to Choose the Best Color for Your Style:

1. **Professional Environments**: If you're using your MacBook Air for work or business purposes, colors like **Space Gray** or **Silver** are ideal for keeping a **professional and polished appearance**.

2. **Personal Aesthetic**: If you want your MacBook to reflect a bit more of your personality, **Starlight** or **Midnight** adds a unique and stylish flair that will stand out in a crowd.

3. **Protecting the Surface**: The colors may slightly impact the **visibility of scratches** or wear over time, with **darker colors** (like **Midnight**) potentially showing marks more than the lighter **Silver** or **Starlight** colors.

Eco-Friendly Materials and Sustainable Manufacturing

The MacBook Air's Commitment to Sustainability: Apple has made significant strides in creating a **more eco-friendly product**. The MacBook Air (M4, 2025) is made with **100% recycled aluminum**, reducing the need for new materials and minimizing the environmental impact of manufacturing.

Maximizing the Sustainability Features:

1. **Recycling Your Device**:

   o   After years of use, when you're ready to upgrade, don't throw your MacBook away. Instead, use Apple's **Trade-In Program** or visit an **Apple Store** to recycle it properly.

   o   If you no longer need it, you can receive **Apple Store credit** for your old MacBook to be reused or refurbished.

2. **Energy Efficiency**:

   o   The **M4 chip** inside the MacBook Air has been designed to **consume less power**, improving energy efficiency without compromising performance. This helps reduce the environmental footprint, especially when charging your MacBook.

13" Retina Display: Resolution, Brightness, and Color Accuracy

Understanding the Display Quality:

1. **13" Retina Display**:

   o   The MacBook Air's **13-inch Retina display** features a **resolution of 2560 x 1600 pixels**, delivering crisp and clear images for all types of content. Whether you're working on **documents, watching movies**, or **editing photos**, the sharpness of the Retina display ensures that everything looks crisp and vivid.

2. **Brightness and Color Accuracy**:

   o With a **maximum brightness of 500 nits**, the MacBook Air's display is perfect for working in **bright environments** or outdoor settings.

   o **P3 wide color gamut** and **True Tone** ensure that the colors you see on the screen are as **accurate as possible**, which is essential for creative professionals like **photographers**, **videographers**, and **designers** who rely on true-to-life color accuracy.

   o **True Tone** adjusts the display's white balance to match the surrounding light, so it's always easier on the eyes.

How to Get the Best Viewing Experience:

1. **Adjusting the Brightness**:

   o You can manually adjust the screen brightness through the **Control Center** or by using the **F1/F2 keys**.

   o Enable **True Tone** in the **Display Preferences** for optimal viewing comfort, especially in different lighting environments.

2. **Optimizing Color Accuracy**:

- If you're involved in any **creative work** that requires precision (like **photo editing** or **video production**), enable the **P3 wide color** profile in your **Display Settings** for the most accurate representation of colors.

- **Use professional calibration tools** if you want even more precise color accuracy for **graphic design** or **video editing**.

Liquid Retina Display Technology and True Tone

The **Liquid Retina** display technology on the MacBook Air (M4, 2025) uses **advanced LCD technology** to deliver **true-to-life visuals**. The **True Tone** feature ensures that the display adjusts to the ambient lighting around you, making it easier to use in varying environments.

To Use the Display for Optimal Comfort:

- Turn on **True Tone** for an automatic adjustment of color temperature based on the surrounding lighting. This will make the screen easier to look at for extended periods.

  If you're using your MacBook in dark settings, it's beneficial to **reduce the brightness** and enable **Night Shift** to reduce blue light exposure, which can help you sleep better.

Magic Keyboard: Comfortable, Quiet, and Precise Typing

The **Magic Keyboard** on the MacBook Air (M4, 2025) features **scissor-switch keys** that are designed to offer **quiet, comfortable, and accurate typing**. The low-profile design ensures that you don't have to press hard to get a response, which is especially useful during long typing sessions.

How to Optimize Typing on the Magic Keyboard:

1. **Typing Comfortably**:

   o Make sure to keep your wrists in a **neutral position** when typing, especially if you're typing for an extended period. This reduces strain and makes typing more comfortable.

   o You can adjust the **keyboard backlight** by using the **F5** and **F6** keys or in the **Control Center** for better visibility in low-light settings.

2. **Customizing Key Shortcuts**:

   o Customize the **keyboard shortcuts** in the **System Preferences > Keyboard** menu to streamline your workflow, especially if you often use specific apps or functions.

Trackpad Customization and Multi-Touch Gestures

The MacBook Air's **Trackpad** is **larger than most competitors**, making it easier to navigate and use gestures.

How to Use the Trackpad Efficiently:

1. **Master Multi-Touch Gestures**:

    o Use the **three-finger swipe** to easily switch between **desktops** or use **Mission Control**.

    o To **zoom in or out** on photos or web pages, use the **pinch-to-zoom** gesture with two fingers.

    o The **two-finger scroll** helps you move up and down through documents or websites smoothly.

2. **Adjusting Trackpad Settings**:

    o Go to **System Preferences > Trackpad** to adjust the **speed** of tracking or enable/disable specific gestures according to your preferences.

3. **Using Trackpad for Precision**:

    o The larger size and **pressure sensitivity** of the trackpad make it ideal for **precise tasks** such as **photo editing** or **design work** where you need accuracy.

Ports and Charging

MagSafe 3 Charging Port and Benefits: The **MagSafe 3** port reintroduces Apple's **magnetic charging** feature. If you accidentally trip over the power cord, the magnet will detach safely without pulling your MacBook down.

How to Use MagSafe Charging Efficiently:

1. **Connect the MagSafe charger**: Simply align the charging cable with the **MagSafe 3 port**, and it will automatically snap into place. You'll see an **LED light** indicating whether your MacBook is charging.

USB-C / Thunderbolt Ports for Speed and Connectivity: The MacBook Air has **two USB-C / Thunderbolt 4 ports** for **super-fast data transfer** and **charging**.

How to Use the Ports for Connectivity:

1. **Fast File Transfers**: You can transfer large files quickly between your MacBook and external drives or devices.

2. **Connecting External Displays**: If you need a **second screen** for productivity or creative work, simply connect the **Thunderbolt 3** port to an **external display** via the appropriate adapter.

Headphone Jack and Compatibility: The **3.5mm headphone jack** ensures you can use **wired headphones** or connect audio devices without requiring an adapter.

External Display Support via Thunderbolt 3/USB-C:

- You can connect an **external monitor or projector** to your MacBook for extended desktop or presentations, ensuring you have enough screen real estate for multitasking.

This step-by-step guide on the **MacBook Air (M4, 2025)** design and build quality ensures you know exactly how to **optimize** your experience with the MacBook's features. Whether you're using it for **work, creative projects**, or **media consumption**, understanding how to use the hardware is key to getting the most out of this device.

PERFORMANCE AND POWER

In this section, we're diving deep into how the **MacBook Air (M4, 2025)** performs, powered by the advanced **M4 chip**, with a focus on performance, battery life, and how the device manages heat. Follow this guide step-by-step to make sure you're getting the most from your MacBook Air.

Inside the M4 Chip: Unmatched Performance

The **M4 chip** is the heart of the MacBook Air. Here's how you can fully benefit from its capabilities:

Step 1: Understanding the M4 Chip Architecture

- **8-Core CPU (Central Processing Unit)**: This is the primary processor of your MacBook Air. The **8-core CPU** consists of:

    o **4 High-Performance Cores**: These cores are dedicated to intensive tasks like video editing or gaming. They work fast and hard when you need power.

    o **4 Efficiency Cores**: These cores handle lighter tasks like web browsing or document editing, saving energy when you're not pushing the system hard.

How to maximize it:

- For everyday use like web browsing or writing, the **efficiency cores** will handle tasks efficiently and conserve battery.

- When using resource-heavy applications (e.g., **Final Cut Pro**, **Photoshop**, or games), the **performance cores** will automatically kick in to ensure smooth performance.

Step 2: Make Use of the 10-Core GPU (Graphics Processing Unit)

The **10-core GPU** takes care of graphics and visual tasks. It's perfect for creative professionals and gamers.

How to benefit from it:

- **Video Editing & Creative Work**: If you're working on 4K video, the GPU will help with faster rendering and smoother playback in editing software like **Final Cut Pro** and **Adobe Premiere**. For a smooth experience, increase your project resolution if you're working with high-definition videos.

- **Gaming**: If you're into gaming, you'll notice the improved graphics rendering when playing graphically demanding games. Set your **in-game resolution** to the highest possible setting for the best experience, but be mindful of performance for longer gaming sessions.

Step 3: Leverage the 16-Core Neural Engine for AI Integration

The **16-core Neural Engine** is responsible for handling artificial intelligence (AI) tasks. This makes everything from voice recognition to facial ID much faster.

How to use it:

- Use **Siri** or **Spotlight Search**: The Neural Engine helps **Siri** understand voice commands faster and more accurately.

- **Image Editing**: When editing photos in apps like **Photoshop** or **Lightroom**, AI-based features like **auto-enhance** or **content-aware fill** are powered by the Neural Engine, making edits faster and more precise.

- **Machine Learning Apps**: If you use apps with AI-based tools, the Neural Engine will improve the overall speed and accuracy.

Battery Life

The **MacBook Air (M4, 2025)** is designed to maximize battery life, making it perfect for long working hours or travel. Here's how you can ensure you get the most battery life:

Step 1: Understanding Battery Life in Different Scenarios

- **Up to 18 Hours of Video Playback**: If you're watching movies or streaming content, the MacBook can last up to **18 hours** on a single charge. This makes it ideal for long flights, extended meetings, or road trips where access to power outlets is limited.

- **Up to 15 Hours of Web Browsing**: For general web browsing (checking emails, surfing the web), the MacBook Air can last up to **15 hours**.

Tip for maximizing battery life:

- Use the MacBook Air's **energy-saving settings** in **System Preferences > Battery**.

- Lower your screen brightness when you're working in low-light environments to save battery.

Step 2: Battery Management Features

- **Battery Health Management**: This feature helps to extend the lifespan of your MacBook's battery by adjusting the maximum charge based on your usage patterns. For instance, if you typically leave your laptop plugged in, this feature will prevent the battery from charging to full 100% all the time, which can degrade battery life over time.

How to enable:

- Go to **System Preferences > Battery > Battery Health** and make sure **Battery health management** is turned on.

Step 3: Best Practices for Charging

- Charge your MacBook Air when the battery dips below **20%**.

- If you're planning on not using your MacBook Air for an extended period, store it with about **50% battery**. This prevents battery degradation.

Thermal Management

The **MacBook Air (M4, 2025)** is fanless, meaning it runs silently. However, it still needs to manage heat efficiently, especially when running demanding applications. Here's how thermal management works:

Step 1: Understanding Fanless Design and Heat Dissipation

The **M4 chip** is built to be efficient with power, which minimizes the heat produced. The MacBook Air uses **passive cooling** techniques, meaning heat is spread evenly across the laptop's body and dissipated naturally through its thin aluminum frame.

What this means for you:

- The MacBook Air remains cool even under moderate loads, so it doesn't produce loud fan noise.

- **No fans** mean less dust accumulation inside the device, keeping it clean and efficient.

Step 2: Silent Performance for Quiet Work Environments

Since there are no fans, the MacBook Air is exceptionally quiet. Whether you're working in a library, coffee shop, or during video calls, you'll never have to worry about fan noise.

How to benefit:

- If you need to record audio or join video conferences, the fanless design ensures that no unwanted noise will interfere with your work.

Step 3: Managing Thermal Performance Under Load

Even though the MacBook Air doesn't have fans, it does need to manage heat when performing **intensive tasks** like gaming or rendering videos. To handle heat, the **M4 chip** and the MacBook's design automatically lower performance to maintain optimal temperature levels, a process known as **thermal throttling**.

How to handle it:

- If you're working with demanding applications, make sure your MacBook is placed on a hard, flat surface to help with heat dissipation.

- You can also **lower the graphical settings** in **games** or **video editing software** to prevent the system from producing excess heat.

To make the most of the **MacBook Air (M4, 2025)**, keep these steps in mind:

1. **Maximize Performance**: Use the **8-core CPU** and **10-core GPU** to their full potential by switching between **high-performance** and **efficiency cores** depending on your tasks.

2. **Optimize Battery Life**: Take advantage of **Low Power Mode** for light tasks, and enable **Battery Health Management** for long-term battery care.

3. **Keep It Cool**: Even though the MacBook Air has no fans, place it on a hard surface and use cooling pads for demanding tasks like gaming or video rendering.

4. **Use AI Features**: Leverage the **16-core Neural Engine** for faster performance in apps that use

machine learning for tasks like photo enhancement and voice recognition.

By following these simple steps, you can ensure that your **MacBook Air (M4, 2025)** remains efficient, powerful, and optimized for your everyday tasks, creative work, or gaming needs. Enjoy the best of performance, portability, and battery life in one sleek package!

SETTING UP YOUR MACBOOK AIR (M4, 2025)

This section provides a step-by-step guide to **unbox**, **set up**, and **personalize** your MacBook Air (M4, 2025) for the first time. We'll also walk you through how to navigate the operating system, **macOS Sonoma**, and how to make the MacBook fit your personal needs.

Unboxing and First-Time Setup

Step 1: Unboxing Your MacBook Air

When you first get your hands on the **MacBook Air (M4, 2025)**, the unboxing experience is straightforward and minimalistic, reflecting Apple's dedication to sleek and eco-friendly design.

Here's what's inside the box:

- **MacBook Air (M4, 2025)**: The main device itself.

- **USB-C Charging Cable**: The cable for charging your MacBook (magnetic MagSafe 3 connector on one side, USB-C on the other).

- **30W USB-C Power Adapter**: The charging brick that connects to the USB-C cable.

- **Documentation**: Includes a small user guide, safety instructions, and Apple stickers.

How to unbox:

1. **Open the Box**: Gently lift the top of the box to reveal the MacBook, which is neatly wrapped in protective plastic. Pull the MacBook out carefully.

2. **Remove Packaging Materials**: Take out the power cable and the charging brick from their compartments.

3. **Keep Everything Organized**: You may want to save the box and packaging materials in case you need to return or store the device.

Step 2: First-Time Setup

Once you've unboxed your MacBook Air, it's time to start setting it up. Follow these instructions to get started:

1. **Powering On the MacBook**:
   - Press and hold the **power button** (on the top-right of the keyboard) to turn on your MacBook Air.
   - The Apple logo will appear on the screen, followed by the welcome screen.

2. **Select Your Language and Region**:
   - Choose your preferred **language** (English, Spanish, French, etc.) and your **region** (e.g., the United States).
   - After selecting these options, click **Continue**.

3. **Connect to Wi-Fi**:

o   You'll be prompted to connect to a Wi-Fi network. Click on your network name, then enter the **password** if necessary.

o   **Tip**: Ensure that your Wi-Fi connection is stable, as this will help you download updates and sign into your Apple ID seamlessly.

4. **Sign into Your Apple ID**:

o   If you already have an Apple ID, **sign in** with your Apple ID credentials (email and password). This will link your MacBook to your **Apple ecosystem**.

o   If you don't have an Apple ID yet, you can create one by selecting **Create New Apple ID**. Follow the on-screen instructions to provide your details, including email, password, and security questions.

Why Sign In?

Signing in with your Apple ID allows you to access a variety of services, including **iCloud** storage, **Apple Music**, **Apple TV**, and more. Your contacts, calendars, and notes will automatically sync across devices.

5. **Setting Up iCloud and Backup**:

o   After signing in, you'll be prompted to enable **iCloud**. iCloud will sync your files, contacts, and other data across Apple devices.

o   You can also enable **iCloud Drive** to store your files safely in the cloud and access them from anywhere.

o   If you have a previous backup (from an old Mac or an iPhone), you can **restore** from iCloud to transfer your old data.

6. **Set Up Touch ID**:

o   The MacBook Air comes with **Touch ID**, which allows you to unlock your MacBook, make purchases, and log into apps with your fingerprint.

o   Follow the instructions to **register your fingerprint** by placing your finger on the **Touch ID sensor** on the top-right of the keyboard.

7. **Set Up Location Services**:

o   Enable **Location Services** to allow apps like **Maps** and **Find My Mac** to access your location. You can choose to turn it off later if you prefer privacy.

8. **Set Up FileVault Encryption**:

o   For security, FileVault encrypts all the files on your MacBook Air. You'll be prompted to turn it on during setup. Enabling FileVault makes your files unreadable to unauthorized people.

9. **Screen Time and Other Preferences**:

o   Set up **Screen Time** if you wish to track and limit your computer usage.

o   You'll also be prompted to adjust some basic **preferences** like privacy settings, data sharing, and diagnostic reporting.

macOS: Introduction and Features

Once your MacBook Air is set up, you'll be introduced to **macOS Sonoma**, Apple's most recent operating system. This new update brings exciting features, improved performance, and enhanced security.

Step 1: macOS Sonoma Overview

1. **The Finder**: The Finder is the file management system on your Mac. It allows you to easily browse and organize files.

    o   **How to use Finder**: Open Finder by clicking the **Finder icon** (the smiling face) in your Dock. From there, you can browse documents, images, and apps.

2. **Spotlight Search**:

    o   **What it is**: Spotlight is a powerful search tool that helps you find documents, apps, emails, and even web results.

    o   **How to use**: Click the **magnifying glass** icon in the top-right corner of the screen or press **Command + Space**. Then type the name of the file or app you want to find.

3. **Dock**:

o **What it is**: The Dock provides quick access to your favorite apps and open windows.

o **How to use**: Drag apps to the Dock for easy access. Right-click on apps to access quick actions (e.g., open a new window, minimize, or close).

o **Customization**: Go to **System Preferences** > **Dock** to adjust size, position, and minimize effects.

4. **Notifications Center**:

o The **Notification Center** allows you to see alerts for new emails, messages, calendar events, and app updates.

o **How to use**: Swipe right from the edge of the trackpad to open the **Notification Center**. Here, you can interact with notifications, or swipe them away.

5. **System Preferences**:

o The **System Preferences** app is where you configure everything on your Mac.

o **How to use**: Access it by clicking on the **Apple Menu** > **System Preferences**. This is where you can customize your Wi-Fi, notifications, and other settings.

Step 2: Key macOS Applications

Here are some essential macOS apps that come pre-installed on your MacBook Air:

1. **Safari**: The default web browser for browsing the internet. It's optimized for speed and security.

   o **How to use**: Launch Safari from your **Dock** or use **Spotlight** to search for it. Use tabs for multitasking and install extensions to enhance browsing.

2. **Mail**: The built-in email app that syncs with your Apple ID and iCloud.

   o **How to use**: Open the **Mail** app, and configure your email account (Gmail, iCloud, etc.) by going to **Mail > Preferences**.

3. **Calendar**: A built-in calendar for managing your appointments and events.

   o **How to use**: Open **Calendar** to create events. You can sync it with your iCloud to keep your events up-to-date across devices.

4. **Messages**: Apple's messaging app for sending SMS and iMessages.

   o **How to use**: Open **Messages** to send and receive text messages. If you have an iPhone, your messages will sync automatically across your Apple devices.

Personalizing Your MacBook Air

Now that your MacBook Air is set up, you can customize the look and feel to match your preferences.

Step 1: Customizing System Preferences and Themes

1. **Change System Appearance**:
   - Go to **System Preferences > General** to toggle between **Light**, **Dark**, or **Auto** modes. Dark mode gives a more subdued aesthetic and saves battery on OLED screens.

2. **Adjust Fonts and Size**:
   - Go to **System Preferences > Accessibility > Display** to increase text size or reduce transparency for easier readability.

3. **Set Up Desktop and Screensavers**:
   - To set a wallpaper, go to **System Preferences > Desktop & Screen Saver**, then choose from the default Apple wallpapers or select your own.

4. **Customize the Dock**:
   - Right-click on the Dock to **resize** or **move** it. You can also choose to hide the Dock when not in use for a cleaner workspace.

Step 2: Using Accessibility Features

1. **VoiceOver**: A screen reader for those with visual impairments. Activate it through **System Preferences > Accessibility > VoiceOver**.

2. **Zoom**: If you have difficulty seeing the screen, you can use the **Zoom** function to enlarge parts of the screen.

3. **Magnification**: Enabling this lets you use your mouse cursor to zoom into the screen by adjusting the **Display** settings under **Accessibility**.

Your **MacBook Air (M4, 2025)** is now ready for use! You've learned how to unbox it, perform the initial setup, explore macOS features, and personalize it to your needs. As you continue to use the device, remember to explore new apps, manage settings, and adjust preferences to optimize your experience

WORKING WITH APPLICATIONS

Built-In Apps

The MacBook Air (M4, 2025) comes with several powerful built-in apps that can help with daily tasks, creative projects, and communication. Let's walk through the key apps, their functionalities, and tips to make the most out of them.

Safari: Fast, Private Browsing

What is Safari? Safari is Apple's built-in web browser designed for fast, secure, and private internet browsing. It supports features like fast page loading, energy efficiency, and privacy protections such as Intelligent Tracking Prevention.

Step 1: Opening Safari

- To start using Safari, click the **Safari icon** on your **Dock**, or press Cmd + Space to open **Spotlight Search**, type "Safari", and hit **Enter**.

Step 2: Navigating Between Tabs

- **Opening a New Tab**: In the upper-right corner of Safari, click the + icon next to your open tabs.

- **Switching Tabs**: Click on any tab at the top to switch between them. For quicker access, use the Ctrl + Tab shortcut to cycle through open tabs.

Step 3: Private Browsing Mode

- To browse without leaving any trace, click **File** in the top menu and select **New Private Window**. You'll see a darkened interface to indicate you're in private mode.

Step 4: Managing Bookmarks

- To save a webpage, click the **Share** button (square with an arrow) in the top menu, then select **Add Bookmark**. You can organize your bookmarks by creating folders.

Step 5: Managing Extensions

- Click **Safari > Preferences > Extensions** to browse and install various extensions like ad blockers or password managers, which enhance your browsing experience.

Mail, Calendar, Contacts: Managing Your Daily Life

What is Mail, Calendar, and Contacts? These built-in apps help you manage your communication and schedule. **Mail** helps you send and receive emails, **Calendar** lets you organize events and appointments, and **Contacts** stores and organizes all your important contact information.

Mail: Managing Emails

Step 1: Opening Mail

- Click the **Mail** icon in your **Dock** or search for it using **Spotlight** (Cmd + Space).

Step 2: Setting Up Your Email Account

- When you first launch Mail, the app will prompt you to add an email account. Select the service (e.g., Gmail, Yahoo) and log in with your credentials.

- To add more accounts later, click **Mail > Accounts** in the menu and follow the on-screen prompts.

Step 3: Composing and Sending Emails

- To write a new email, click the **New Message** button (or use the shortcut Cmd + N). Enter the recipient's address, subject, and body.

- **Attachments**: To attach files, click the **paperclip icon** or drag and drop the file into the email body.

Step 4: Organizing Emails

- Use **Folders** and **Smart Mailboxes** to organize your emails. To create a new folder, go to **Mailbox > New Mailbox**.

Calendar: Scheduling and Organizing Your Time

Step 1: Opening Calendar

- Click on the **Calendar** icon in the **Dock** or use **Spotlight** (Cmd + Space) to find it.

Step 2: Adding an Event

- To add an event, double-click on the desired date or click the + button at the top-right of the window. A dialog box will appear, prompting you to enter the event's details (time, location, notes).

Step 3: Syncing with iCloud

- To sync your calendar across devices, ensure you're signed into **iCloud**. Go to **System Preferences > Apple ID** and ensure **iCloud** is enabled for Calendar.

Step 4: Setting Reminders for Events

- When creating an event, you can set an alert by clicking the **Add Alert** button, which will notify you ahead of time via a pop-up, email, or sound

Contacts: Managing Your Connections

Step 1: Opening Contacts

- Open **Contacts** from your **Dock** or search using **Spotlight** (Cmd + Space).

Step 2: Adding New Contacts

- Click the + button at the bottom-left to add a new contact. You can enter information like name, email, phone number, and even social media handles.

Step 3: Syncing with iCloud

- Just like your Calendar, Contacts can be synced across all your Apple devices. Ensure **iCloud Contacts** is enabled in **System Preferences > Apple ID**.

Productivity Apps for Business

What are Pages, Numbers, and Keynote? Pages, Numbers, and Keynote are Apple's alternatives to Microsoft Word, Excel, and PowerPoint. These apps are designed for creating documents, spreadsheets, and presentations, respectively, and they work seamlessly across all your Apple devices with iCloud sync.

Pages: Document Creation

Step 1: Opening Pages

- Open **Pages** by clicking its icon in the **Dock** or by searching for it using **Spotlight** (Cmd + Space).

Step 2: Starting a New Document

- Click **New Document**, then choose from various templates (e.g., **Blank**, **Resumé**, **Newsletter**).

- To create a blank document, select **Blank** and begin typing.

Step 3: Formatting and Styling

- Use the top toolbar to format text, adjust font size, and apply styles. You can insert tables, images, and hyperlinks using the **Insert** menu.

Step 4: Sharing and Collaborating

- To share the document with others, click the **Share** button at the top-right and select **Collaborate with Others** via **iCloud**. This allows multiple people to edit the document in real-time.

Numbers: Spreadsheets for Organizing Data

Step 1: Opening Numbers

- Launch **Numbers** from the **Dock** or **Spotlight**.

Step 2: Creating a New Spreadsheet

- Click **New Document**, select a template (e.g., **Budget**, **Personal Finance**), or choose **Blank**.

Step 3: Entering Data

- Type your data directly into the cells. Numbers support basic mathematical functions such as addition (+), subtraction (-), multiplication (*), and division (/).

Step 4: Adding Charts and Graphs

- To visualize your data, select your table or chart area and click on the **Chart** button in the top toolbar. Choose a chart style (e.g., bar, pie, line) and Numbers will generate a visual representation.

Step 5: Sharing and Collaborating

- Like in Pages, click the **Share** button at the top-right, then select **Collaborate**. You can send an email link to allow others to view or edit your spreadsheet in **real-time**.

Keynote: Creating Stunning Presentations

Step 1: Opening Keynote

- Open **Keynote** from the **Dock** or via **Spotlight**.

Step 2: Creating a Presentation

- Click **New Document**, then select a template that suits your presentation style.

Step 3: Adding Content

- Insert **text**, **images**, and **videos** by selecting **Insert** from the top menu. You can add transitions, animations, and other multimedia content to enhance your slides.

Step 4: Presenting Your Work

- Once your slides are ready, click the **Play** button in the top-left corner to view your presentation.

Step 5: Sharing and Collaborating

- To share your presentation, click the **Share** button at the top-right and select **Collaborate** to work with others in real-time.

Media Creation

What are GarageBand, iMovie, and Final Cut Pro X? These apps are designed for creating and editing media. **GarageBand** is a beginner-friendly music creation tool, **iMovie** is for video editing, and **Final Cut Pro X** is a professional video editing software. Together, they allow you to produce music, videos, and more.

GarageBand: Music Creation for Beginners

Step 1: Opening GarageBand

- Open **GarageBand** from the **Dock** or use **Spotlight**.

Step 2: Starting a New Project

- Click **New Project** and select a template (e.g., **Piano**, **Guitar**, or **Voice**). GarageBand will automatically set up your workspace for the selected instrument.

Step 3: Recording Music

- Plug in any instruments you want to use (such as a guitar or keyboard). Press the **Record** button (red circle) in the top toolbar to start recording your track.

Step 4: Editing Your Track

- Click on a recorded section, and you can **cut**, **copy**, or **trim** it. Use the **Track Editor** to add effects like **reverb**, **delay**, and more.

Step 5: Exporting Your Music

- Once done, click **Share > Export Song to Disk** to save your creation. You can also directly upload it to **iTunes** or **SoundCloud**.

iMovie: Simple Video Editing for Beginners

Step 1: Opening iMovie

- Open **iMovie** from the **Dock** or **Spotlight**.

Step 2: Creating a New Project

- Select **Create New > Movie** to start a new project.

Step 3: Importing Footage

- Drag and drop your video clips from **Finder** into the **Timeline** at the bottom of the iMovie interface.

Step 4: Editing Your Video

- Use tools to **cut**, **crop**, and **adjust the speed** of your clips. Add transitions by dragging them between clips.

Step 5: Adding Music and Effects

- Use the **Audio** tab to add background music, sound effects, or voiceovers.

- Apply **visual effects** from the **Effects** tab to enhance your video.

Step 6: Exporting Your Video

- When you're happy with your video, click the **Export** button in the top-right corner and choose your export settings (file type, resolution).

Productivity with Microsoft 365 and Google Apps

What is Microsoft 365 and Google Apps? Microsoft 365 includes apps like Word, Excel, and PowerPoint, while Google Apps (Docs, Sheets, and Slides) offer similar features, all accessible in the cloud. Both suites allow you to create, edit, and share documents across devices.

Using Microsoft Office Apps

Step 1: Installing Microsoft 365

- Download and install Microsoft 365 from the **Mac App Store** or the official **Microsoft website**.

Step 2: Creating and Editing Documents

- Open **Word, Excel**, or **PowerPoint** and start a new file or open an existing one. Use the toolbar for formatting and editing.

Using Google Apps in a Web Browser

Step 1: Access Google Apps

- Visit **docs.google.com, sheets.google.com**, or **slides.google.com** in your browser to use Google Docs, Sheets, and Slides directly.

Step 2: Creating and Editing Files

- Open **Google Docs** to start a new document or **Google Sheets** to create a new spreadsheet. You can collaborate in real-time by clicking the **Share** button in the upper-right corner.

Step 3: Syncing Files

- As long as you're logged into your **Google account**, your documents will automatically sync across all your devices, making them accessible anytime, anywhere.

By following these step-by-step instructions, you'll quickly get the hang of using essential apps like Safari for browsing, Mail for staying in touch, Pages for writing documents, and GarageBand for making music. Each guide is designed to help you understand exactly what each app can do and how you can make the most of it— whether you're getting work done, creating something awesome, or collaborating with others.

STORAGE, BACKUPS, AND FILE MANAGEMENT

Storage Options

Choosing the right storage for your MacBook Air is crucial to ensure you have enough space for your files, apps, and media. The MacBook Air (M4, 2025) offers four different storage options: 256GB, 512GB, 1TB, and 2TB. Below is a guide on how to make the best choice and how to manage your files effectively once you've selected your storage.

Step 1: Choosing the Right Storage Size

256GB Storage

- **Best For:** Light users who mainly use web browsers, email, and a few essential apps. This size is ideal if you prefer to store most of your files in the cloud.

- **How to Maximize Space:** Use cloud services like iCloud to offload documents and photos. You can also use external hard drives for larger files or projects you don't need on a daily basis.

512GB Storage

- **Best For:** Everyday users who need to store a moderate amount of files, including documents, photos, and videos. This option is suitable if you plan on installing several apps, but you still rely on cloud storage for large media libraries.

- **How to Maximize Space:** Organize your files using Finder and offload your large media files (like videos and music) to cloud storage or an external drive when you're not using them.

1TB Storage

- **Best For:** Users who work with large files frequently—like business professionals, designers, or photographers. This configuration is perfect for those who need plenty of local storage to hold video files, high-resolution images, and large apps.

- **How to Maximize Space:** Consider using Time Machine for backups and offloading less frequently used files to an external SSD or cloud services like iCloud for easy access.

2TB Storage

- **Best For:** Power users or creators with high-performance needs. If you frequently handle massive video editing projects, 3D modeling, or large-scale media libraries, this configuration will provide the ample storage space you need.

- **How to Maximize Space:** Use the **Optimize Mac Storage** feature in iCloud to move your older files to the cloud, freeing up local storage without losing access to them.

Step 2: Managing Files on macOS

macOS has a streamlined file management system that makes it easy to store, organize, and find your files.

1. **Using Finder to Organize Files**
   Finder is the built-in file management tool for macOS. Here's how to use it effectively:

   - **Opening Finder:** Click the **Finder** icon in your Dock (smiling face).

   - **Creating Folders:** To create a new folder, click on **File** in the top menu and select **New Folder**, or right-click in any open Finder window and choose **New Folder**.

   - **Using Tags:** To quickly organize files, you can assign **tags** (colored labels) to them. Right-click on a file, select **Tags**, and choose a color or label. You can later sort or search for files using these tags.

2. **Local vs. iCloud Storage**

   - **Local Storage:** Files saved on your Mac are stored locally on your SSD. While this gives you fast access to files, you'll eventually run out of space if you store too many large files.

   - **iCloud Storage:** iCloud Drive offers a way to store files in the cloud, freeing up space on your device while keeping your files accessible from all your Apple devices. Files you save to iCloud are synced across your Mac, iPhone, iPad, and even accessible on the web through **iCloud.com**.

iCloud and File Management

iCloud is Apple's cloud storage service, and it integrates seamlessly into macOS. It allows you to store files in the cloud, sync them across all your devices, and free up space on your Mac. Here's how to set up iCloud and manage your files.

Step 1: Setting Up iCloud Drive

1. **Enable iCloud on Your Mac**

   o Open **System Preferences** by clicking the **Apple menu** in the top-left corner of your screen.

   o Select **Apple ID**, then click **iCloud** in the sidebar.

   o Check the box next to **iCloud Drive** to enable it.

   o After enabling iCloud Drive, you'll be able to store files in the cloud, keeping them synced across your devices.

2. **Accessing iCloud Files**

   o **Finder:** Open Finder, and in the sidebar, you'll see **iCloud Drive** listed. Click on it to see all the files and folders stored in iCloud.

   o **File Uploading:** To store a file in iCloud, simply drag it into the **iCloud Drive** section in Finder, or use the **Save As** option in any app to select iCloud as the destination.

Step 2: Managing iCloud Storage

1. **Optimizing Storage**

    o   Go to **System Preferences** > **Apple ID** > **iCloud** and click **Options** next to **iCloud Drive**.

    o   Enable **Optimize Mac Storage**, which will automatically store older files in iCloud and keep only recent files on your Mac. This saves space on your local storage without losing access to your files.

2. **Checking iCloud Storage**

    o   Open **System Preferences**, then click **Apple ID** > **iCloud**.

    o   You can see how much iCloud storage is being used and what is consuming it. If you're running low on space, you can upgrade your plan directly from here.

Backup and Recovery

Backups are essential for ensuring that you don't lose your important files. Time Machine, Apple's built-in backup software, allows you to automatically back up your Mac to an external hard drive, network drive, or other storage device. Here's how to set it up and use it to restore your files or system.

Step 1: Setting Up Time Machine for Automatic Backups

1. **Connect an External Drive**

    o   Plug in an external hard drive (preferably 1TB or more) to your Mac. This will be used as your backup disk.

    o   A prompt will appear asking if you want to use this drive with Time Machine. Select **Use as Backup Disk**.

2. **Activate Time Machine**

    o   Open **System Preferences** and select **Time Machine**.

    o   Toggle the switch to **On**.

    o   Time Machine will automatically back up your system every hour, keeping hourly backups for the last 24 hours, daily backups for the past month, and weekly backups for all previous months.

Step 2: Restoring Files and Data from Time Machine

1. **Restoring Files**

    o   Click the **Time Machine icon** in the menu bar (it looks like a clock with an arrow around it).

    o   Use the **Timeline** on the right side of the screen to scroll back to the time you want to restore from.

o Select the file(s) or folder(s) you want to restore, and click **Restore**.

2. **Restoring Your Entire System**

   o If you need to restore your entire system, restart your Mac and hold down **Command + R** to enter **macOS Recovery Mode**.

   o Once in Recovery Mode, select **Restore from Time Machine Backup** and follow the on-screen instructions to restore your system.

Step 3: Using macOS Recovery for Troubleshooting

1. **Reinstall macOS**

   o If your Mac isn't working properly and you want to reinstall macOS, you can do this from **macOS Recovery**.

   o Restart your Mac and hold down **Command + R**.

   o Select **Reinstall macOS** and follow the instructions to download and install the latest version of macOS.

2. **Repairing Your Disk with Disk Utility**

   o In **macOS Recovery**, select **Disk Utility** to repair your disk if you're experiencing issues.

o   Choose your disk from the sidebar and click **First Aid** to scan and repair any disk errors.

By following these steps, you will have a comprehensive understanding of how to manage your MacBook Air's storage, use iCloud effectively to keep files synced across devices, and set up backups to protect your important data. These tools and strategies will ensure you have a smooth, efficient experience with your MacBook Air and prevent data loss due to unforeseen circumstances.

CONNECTIVITY AND ECOSYSTEM INTEGRATION

Wi-Fi, Bluetooth, and Networking

Connecting to Wi-Fi Networks and Troubleshooting

1. **Connecting to a Wi-Fi Network:**

   o **Step 1:** Click the **Wi-Fi icon** located in the top-right corner of the menu bar on your MacBook Air.

   o **Step 2:** A dropdown menu will appear showing all available Wi-Fi networks.

   o **Step 3:** Select your preferred Wi-Fi network from the list. If the network is password-protected, a prompt will appear asking for the Wi-Fi password.

   o **Step 4:** Enter the password and click **Join**. Your MacBook will connect to the network, and the Wi-Fi icon will turn solid to indicate a successful connection.

2. **Troubleshooting Wi-Fi Issues:**

   o **Step 1:** If your MacBook cannot connect to Wi-Fi, first check if other devices (like your phone or another computer) can connect to the same network. If they can, the issue might be specific to your MacBook.

- o **Step 2:** Click the **Wi-Fi icon**, select **Turn Wi-Fi Off**, wait for a few seconds, and then turn it back on.

- o **Step 3:** If that doesn't help, try clicking **Open Network Preferences** from the Wi-Fi dropdown, and under the **Advanced** section, you can **forget the network** and reconnect to it.

- o **Step 4:** If issues persist, try resetting your router or contacting your network provider for support.

Pairing Bluetooth Devices

Bluetooth connectivity on the MacBook Air allows you to connect wireless peripherals, such as a mouse, keyboard, headphones, or speakers. Here's how to pair Bluetooth devices:

1. **Step 1:** Click the **Apple Menu** (top-left corner) and select **System Preferences**.

2. **Step 2:** In the **System Preferences** window, click on **Bluetooth**. Make sure Bluetooth is turned **On**.

3. **Step 3:** Put your Bluetooth device into pairing mode. For example:

   - o **Headphones:** Hold the power button until the light flashes or until you hear a prompt saying "Pairing mode."

   - o **Keyboard/Mouse:** Press and hold the **pairing button** (usually indicated with a Bluetooth logo or marked as such).

4. **Step 4:** Once your device appears in the list on your MacBook, click **Connect** next to its name.

5. **Step 5:** Follow any on-screen instructions that may appear, such as entering a passcode for security or confirming the connection.

6. **Step 6:** Once connected, the device will show up in the list of paired devices in Bluetooth preferences.

Troubleshooting Bluetooth Pairing:

- If a Bluetooth device isn't connecting, try turning the device off and on, or restarting your MacBook Air.

- Ensure there's no interference from other wireless devices and that your MacBook is within range of the Bluetooth device.

Using USB-C, Thunderbolt, and AirDrop for File Transfers

1. **USB-C and Thunderbolt:**

   o **Step 1:** Plug in your **USB-C** or **Thunderbolt** device (like an external hard drive, dock, or USB stick) into one of the Thunderbolt/USB-C ports on your MacBook Air.

   o **Step 2:** macOS will automatically detect the device, and it should appear in **Finder** under the **Devices** section.

o **Step 3:** From Finder, you can drag and drop files to/from the device for easy file management.

o **Step 4:** If you want to safely eject the device, right-click its name in Finder and choose **Eject** before physically disconnecting it.

2. **AirDrop for File Transfers:**

o **Step 1:** Open **Finder** on your MacBook Air and select **AirDrop** from the left sidebar. Ensure that both Bluetooth and Wi-Fi are turned on.

o **Step 2:** On the recipient device (iPhone, iPad, or another Mac), open **AirDrop** and make sure it is discoverable.

o **Step 3:** From Finder on your MacBook Air, drag the files you want to send onto the AirDrop window.

o **Step 4:** You'll see a list of nearby devices. Choose the device you want to send files to.

o **Step 5:** Accept the file transfer on the recipient device to complete the process.

Working with iPhone, iPad, and Apple Watch

Using Handoff and Continuity for Seamless Workflow

Handoff and Continuity are features that let you start an activity on one Apple device and continue it on another, ensuring a smooth workflow between your devices.

1. **Step 1:** Make sure that **Bluetooth** and **Wi-Fi** are enabled on all devices (MacBook Air, iPhone, iPad, or Apple Watch).

2. **Step 2:** Sign in to all devices with the same **Apple ID**.

3. **Step 3:** On your MacBook, begin working in an app that supports Handoff, such as Safari or Pages.

4. **Step 4:** On your iPhone or iPad, you should see an app icon in the **app switcher** (swipe up from the bottom of the screen) showing the activity you can continue.

5. **Step 5:** Click on the app icon to pick up where you left off.

Examples:

- **Safari:** Start reading an article on your Mac, and continue reading it on your iPhone by clicking the Safari icon in the iPhone's app switcher.

- **Mail:** Start composing an email on your iPad, and finish it on your MacBook Air using Handoff.

Using AirDrop for Quick File Transfers Between Apple Devices

AirDrop is an easy way to send files between Apple devices. Here's how to use it:

1. **Step 1:** Open **Finder** on your MacBook Air and click on **AirDrop** in the left sidebar.

2. **Step 2:** On your iPhone or iPad, open the **Share** menu (the box with an arrow) when viewing a file, image, or webpage.

3. **Step 3:** From the Share menu, tap the **AirDrop** icon.

4. **Step 4:** Your MacBook should appear in the list of devices, and you can select it to send the file.

5. **Step 5:** Accept the file on your Mac to begin the transfer.

Syncing Your Mac with Apple Watch for Health, Notifications, and Security

Your Apple Watch can work seamlessly with your MacBook to provide enhanced functionality and security features.

1. **Step 1:** Pair your Apple Watch with your iPhone by following the on-screen instructions in the **Apple Watch app**.

2. **Step 2:** On your Mac, enable **Unlock with Apple Watch** for enhanced security:

   o Open **System Preferences** on your Mac.

   o Click **Security & Privacy** and check the box next to **Use your Apple Watch to unlock apps and your Mac**.

3. **Step 3:** To view health data synced from your iPhone to your Apple Watch, open the **Health**

app on your iPhone. Your MacBook will automatically sync health data if the apps support it.

4. **Step 4:** Set up **Notifications** from your Mac to appear on your Apple Watch, allowing you to keep track of updates without checking your Mac directly.

Using External Displays and Accessories

Connecting to External Monitors via USB-C/Thunderbolt

The MacBook Air supports external displays for an enhanced multi-monitor setup, allowing you to boost productivity. Here's how to set up an external display:

1. **Step 1:** Connect the external monitor to your MacBook Air using a **USB-C** or **Thunderbolt** cable (you may need an adapter depending on the display's port type).

2. **Step 2:** The MacBook will automatically detect the display and extend or mirror the screen. If the display doesn't show up, open **System Preferences** > **Displays**, then click **Detect Displays**.

3. **Step 3:** Adjust the display settings such as resolution, color, and display arrangement in the **Displays** settings to optimize your workflow.

4. **Step 4:** To extend your desktop, drag windows across the edges of your screen. To mirror your display, select the **Mirror Displays** checkbox.

Recommended External Accessories

1. **Keyboards and Mice:**

   o You can pair a **Bluetooth keyboard** or **mouse** to your MacBook Air as described in the Bluetooth section.

   o For wired accessories, simply plug them into a USB-C port using the appropriate adapters.

2. **Headphones and Audio Equipment:**

   o Use the **Bluetooth** section of **System Preferences** to pair wireless headphones, speakers, or other audio devices.

   o For wired headphones, plug them into the **headphone jack** or connect via USB-C adapters.

Setting Up Multi-Screen Workspaces for Increased Productivity

1. **Step 1:** With the external monitor connected, arrange your screens for better multitasking:

   o Go to **System Preferences** > **Displays** > **Arrangement**.

   o Drag the display icons to align them according to your desk layout.

2. **Step 2:** You can set one display as the **primary screen** (where the menu bar and dock appear) by dragging the white bar to the desired monitor.

3. **Step 3:** Use **Mission Control** (swipe up with three fingers) to manage open windows on multiple displays. You can also drag windows from one screen to another by clicking and holding on the window's title bar.

This section offers all the details you need to seamlessly connect your MacBook Air with the Apple ecosystem and external devices. Whether you're connecting to a Wi-Fi network, pairing Bluetooth devices, or syncing with your iPhone and Apple Watch, you now have the tools and knowledge to take full advantage of the MacBook Air's connectivity features.

SECURITY AND PRIVACY

This section will guide you through how to secure your MacBook Air and protect your data, including setting up Touch ID, enabling two-factor authentication for your Apple ID, managing privacy settings, and more. These steps are for users who may not have used these features before, so I'll explain each part clearly.

Touch ID and Secure Enclave

Touch ID allows you to unlock your MacBook Air, make payments, and securely sign into apps with just your fingerprint. It's simple to set up and very convenient. Let's walk through the steps of setting it up:

How to Set Up Touch ID:

1. **Open System Settings**:

   o Click on the **Apple logo** in the top-left corner of your screen.

   o From the drop-down menu, select **System Settings**.

2. **Go to Touch ID Settings**:

   o In the System Settings window, find and click on **Touch ID & Password** under the "Privacy & Security" section on the left.

3. **Add a Fingerprint**:

o Click **Add Fingerprint**. You'll be asked to place your finger on the **Touch ID sensor** at the top-right corner of the keyboard.

o Gently press your finger on the sensor. Follow the on-screen prompts to adjust your finger placement and continue until your fingerprint is fully scanned.

4. **Complete the Setup**:

o After scanning, you can choose to use your fingerprint to unlock your Mac, make payments in the App Store, and more. Simply check the options you prefer, and click **Done**.

What's Secure Enclave?

- The **Secure Enclave** is a special part of your Mac's M4 chip that stores your fingerprint data securely. This ensures your fingerprint information is encrypted and protected from unauthorized access. No one, including Apple, can see your fingerprint data.

Apple ID and Two-Factor Authentication

Your **Apple ID** is what connects all your Apple services and data. To keep your Apple ID secure, Apple offers **Two-Factor Authentication (2FA)**. This means that even if someone knows your password, they won't be able to access your account without a second verification step.

How to Set Up Two-Factor Authentication:

1. **Go to System Settings**:

   o Click on the **Apple logo** in the top-left corner of your screen and select **System Settings**.

2. **Click on Your Apple ID**:

   o In the System Settings window, click on your **Apple ID** at the top of the sidebar.

3. **Enable Two-Factor Authentication**:

   o Under the **Security** section, you'll see an option for **Two-Factor Authentication**. If it's not already turned on, click the **Turn On** button.

   o You'll be asked to enter a trusted **phone number** where you can receive verification codes.

4. **Enter the Verification Code**:

   o Apple will send a **code** to your phone. Enter that code on your MacBook to verify your number and complete the setup.

What is Two-Factor Authentication?

- When you sign in to your Apple ID on a new device, Apple will ask for a **verification code** sent to your trusted phone or device. This helps keep your account safe because even if someone has your password, they can't access your account without that second code.

Privacy Settings

Apple makes it easy to control what information apps and websites can access. You can limit the data shared with apps and manage permissions to ensure your privacy.

How to Control App Permissions:

1. **Open System Settings**:

   o Click on the **Apple logo** and select **System Settings**.

2. **Go to Privacy & Security**:

   o Scroll down and click on **Privacy & Security** from the list on the left.

3. **Manage App Permissions**:

   o Under this section, you'll see different categories like **Location Services**, **Camera**, **Microphone**, and more. You can control which apps are allowed to access these features by turning them on or off.

      ▪ For example, if you don't want an app to access your camera, simply toggle the switch next to **Camera** to turn it off for that app.

4. **Manage Tracking**:

o   Scroll down to **Tracking**. Here you can control whether apps can track your activities across other websites and apps. You can toggle this setting off to prevent apps from tracking you.

Why is Privacy Important?

- Controlling app permissions helps protect your personal data. Limiting access to your camera, microphone, and location keeps sensitive information safe.

Find My Mac

Find My Mac is a valuable tool that allows you to locate your MacBook if it's lost or stolen. You can track its location, remotely lock it, or erase your data to protect your privacy.

How to Set Up Find My Mac:

1. **Open System Settings**:

   o   Click on the **Apple logo** and choose **System Settings**.

2. **Go to Apple ID Settings**:

   o   Click on your **Apple ID** at the top of the System Settings sidebar.

3. **Enable Find My Mac**:

   o   In the **iCloud** section, you'll see the option for **Find My Mac**. Toggle the switch to turn it on.

o Make sure **Location Services** are enabled as well, as Find My Mac needs access to your location to track your device.

4. **Verify Location Access**:

o You may need to confirm that your location is accessible for Find My Mac to track the device. This is typically done automatically when you enable the feature.

What Can You Do with Find My Mac?

- **Track Your Mac**: You can use the **Find My** app on another Apple device or log in to **iCloud.com** to view your Mac's location on a map.

- **Activate Lost Mode**: If you've misplaced your MacBook, you can turn on **Lost Mode** to display a message with your contact info on the screen.

- **Erase Your Mac**: If you believe your Mac is lost for good, you can remotely **erase all data** from your device to protect sensitive information.

By following these steps, you will ensure your MacBook Air is fully protected and your privacy is respected. Setting up **Touch ID**, enabling **Two-Factor Authentication**, managing your **Privacy Settings**, and using **Find My Mac** are essential for keeping your data safe from unauthorized access.

These features give you peace of mind, knowing that your MacBook is secure and your personal information is protected. Whether you're using it for everyday tasks or sensitive work, these steps are vital in maintaining a secure digital experience.

You're all set! If you ever need additional help or have questions, feel free to refer back to this guide or reach out to Apple's support. With these security features in place, your MacBook Air will serve you well for years to come.

MAINTENANCE AND LONGEVITY

Regular maintenance and care are crucial for keeping your MacBook Air in top condition. This section covers system maintenance, battery care, and storage management to help you get the most out of your device over time.

System Maintenance

To keep your MacBook Air performing at its best, it's essential to follow a few regular maintenance practices. This includes updating your system, troubleshooting performance issues, and properly caring for your Mac.

How to Keep Your MacBook Air Running Smoothly with Regular Updates:

1. **Open System Settings**:

   - Click the **Apple logo** in the top-left corner of your screen and select **System Settings**.

2. **Check for Software Updates**:

   - In the System Settings menu, scroll down and click on **General**.

   - Click on **Software Update**. Here, you can see if there are any new updates available.

3. **Enable Automatic Updates** (Recommended):

o To ensure your MacBook stays up-to-date without needing to manually check for updates, toggle on **Automatically keep my Mac up to date**. This will allow macOS to download and install important updates on its own.

4. **Install the Update**:

o If an update is available, simply click **Update Now**. Make sure your MacBook is plugged into a charger before installing updates, especially major ones, as they may take longer.

Why Updates are Important:

- Updates bring essential security patches, new features, and performance improvements. Keeping your system updated is one of the best ways to ensure your Mac runs smoothly and securely.

Troubleshooting Common Performance Issues:

If you notice that your MacBook is running slower than usual or if apps are misbehaving, here are a few steps to troubleshoot:

1. **Restart Your Mac**:

o A simple restart can often solve minor glitches and speed up your MacBook. Click the **Apple logo** in the top-left corner and select **Restart**.

2. **Close Unnecessary Applications**:

  o Too many open applications can slow down your Mac. To close an app, click on its window and press **Command + Q**, or right-click the app in the dock and select **Quit**.

3. **Check Activity Monitor**:

  o Open **Activity Monitor** from **Applications > Utilities**. This shows which processes are consuming a lot of resources (CPU, memory). If you find any apps using excessive resources, close them by selecting the app and clicking the **Stop** button (the octagon with an X).

4. **Free Up Disk Space**:

  o Running low on disk space can make your Mac slower. We'll go over how to manage storage in the next section.

5. **Run Disk Utility**:

  o Open **Disk Utility** from **Applications > Utilities**. Select your Mac's hard drive (usually called **Macintosh HD**) and click **First Aid** to check for disk errors and repair them.

Cleaning and Caring for Your MacBook Air:

1. **Clean the Keyboard and Screen**:

  o Turn off your MacBook and use a microfiber cloth to gently wipe the screen and keyboard. Avoid using paper towels or rough materials that might scratch the surface.

- o For stubborn spots, slightly dampen the cloth with water or a mix of water and a small amount of mild dish soap, but never apply liquid directly to your MacBook.

2. **Keep It in a Safe, Cool Environment**:

- o Store your MacBook on a flat surface and avoid placing it near heat sources like radiators or in direct sunlight.

- o If you're not using your MacBook for an extended period, store it in a cool, dry place, and ensure it's powered off to save battery life.

Battery Care and Health

Your MacBook Air's battery is an important component that powers your device. Here's how to maximize its lifespan and maintain battery health.

Tips for Extending Battery Life and Optimizing Performance:

1. **Adjust Screen Brightness**:

- o One of the most effective ways to save battery life is by lowering the screen brightness. Use the **F1** and **F2** keys on your keyboard to adjust brightness manually or go to **System Settings > Displays** to change it.

2. **Enable Battery Saving Features**:

    o In **System Settings**, click **Battery**.

    o Enable **Low Power Mode** to extend battery life when it's running low, or activate **Battery Health Management** to optimize battery charging and extend its lifespan.

3. **Use Energy Saver Settings**:

    o In **Battery Settings**, you can choose to have your MacBook Air automatically go to sleep when inactive. This can help conserve battery life, especially if you forget to turn off your device.

4. **Close Unnecessary Apps and Background Processes**:

    o As mentioned earlier, closing unused apps and disabling background processes will also help reduce the strain on your battery.

Checking Battery Health and Troubleshooting Battery Issues:

1. **Check Battery Health**:

    o Click the **Apple logo**, select **About This Mac**, and go to the **System Report**.

    o Under the **Power** section, check the **Battery Health** information. If it says **Normal**, your battery is in good condition.

- o If it says **Service Battery**, your battery may be degrading and may need replacement.

2. **Troubleshoot Battery Issues**:

   - o If your MacBook Air isn't holding a charge properly, try the following:

     - ▪ Reset the **System Management Controller (SMC)** by turning off your Mac, then pressing and holding **Shift** + **Control** + **Option** on the left side of your keyboard, and pressing the **power button** for 10 seconds. Release all keys and turn your Mac on.

     - ▪ If the issue persists, consider visiting an Apple Store or contacting support.

Storage Management

Keeping your MacBook Air's storage organized and optimized ensures it runs smoothly and avoids unnecessary slowdowns.

How to Monitor Storage Space and Free Up Unused Files:

1. **Check Available Storage**:

   - o Click on the **Apple logo** and go to **About This Mac** > **Storage**. Here, you'll see a visual representation of how much space is used and available on your Mac.

2. **Identify Large Files and Apps**:

   o In the **Storage** tab, click **Manage**. This will bring up a list of large files, apps, and other items taking up space.

   o You can delete unnecessary apps, files, or move them to an external hard drive.

3. **Delete Unnecessary Files**:

   o Go through your **Downloads**, **Documents**, and **Movies** folders to find old or unused files.

   o Drag items you no longer need to the **Trash** and then **Empty Trash** to free up space.

Using Disk Utility for Maintenance and Repair:

1. **Open Disk Utility**:

   o Go to **Applications > Utilities > Disk Utility**.

2. **Run First Aid**:

   o In Disk Utility, select your main disk (usually called **Macintosh HD**) and click the **First Aid** button. This tool checks for any disk errors and repairs them if necessary.

o It's a good idea to run **First Aid** once in a while to maintain the health of your disk.

3. **Manage Storage with macOS Optimizations**:

o In **System Settings > Apple ID > iCloud**, you can choose to store files, photos, and documents in iCloud to free up space on your MacBook.

o You can also use **Optimize Mac Storage** to automatically remove older files from your MacBook that are already stored in iCloud.

By following these maintenance and care tips, your MacBook Air will continue to run efficiently for years. Regular software updates, battery optimization, and proper storage management are key to ensuring that your MacBook stays in great shape. Take the time to check for updates, monitor battery health, and clean out unnecessary files every so often—it will pay off in the long run.

This guide should help you maintain your MacBook Air's performance and ensure it lasts for years, giving you the best experience possible with your device.

ADVANCED FEATURES AND CUSTOMIZATION

macOS Advanced Features

macOS offers a variety of powerful features that allow you to automate tasks, create custom shortcuts, and personalize your system. Here's how to access and use some of these advanced tools.

Using Automator for Task Automation:

Automator is a built-in macOS application that allows you to automate repetitive tasks on your Mac. It's great for saving time and streamlining your workflow.

1. **Open Automator**:

   o Press **Command + Space** to open **Spotlight** search and type **Automator**. Press **Enter** to open the app.

2. **Create a New Workflow**:

   o When Automator opens, click on **New Document**.

   o You can choose between various types of workflows (like **Application**, **Service**, **Quick Action**, etc.). For simple tasks, choose **Quick Action** or **Workflow**.

3. **Add Actions**:

   o On the left-hand side, you will see a list of actions you can add to your workflow.

For example, you could choose **Files &
Folders** to create a task that renames files
in a specific folder.

- o To add an action, simply drag it to the
  workflow area on the right.

4. **Run the Workflow**:

- o After you've set up the actions, click **Run**
  in the top-right corner to execute your
  workflow.

- o If you want the workflow to be available
  later, save it as an application or quick
  action.

5. **Use Automator for Specific Tasks**:

- o Automator can help you automate tasks
  such as:

  - Renaming batches of files.

  - Organizing photos in specific
    folders.

  - Converting file types (e.g.,
    turning PNG images into JPEG).

- o Explore different actions within
  Automator for more automation
  possibilities.

**Creating Custom Shortcuts and Hotkeys for
Efficiency:**

1. **Open System Settings**:

o   Click on the **Apple logo** in the top-left corner and go to **System Settings**.

2. **Navigate to Keyboard Shortcuts**:

o   Select **Keyboard** from the left sidebar, then click on **Shortcuts**.

3. **Add or Modify Shortcuts**:

o   To create a new shortcut, click **App Shortcuts** on the left and then click the + button.

o   You'll need to choose the application for which you want to create a shortcut (e.g., Safari, Finder), then enter the exact menu name of the action you want to trigger (e.g., "New Tab" in Safari) and the keyboard combination you want to assign.

4. **Use System-wide Shortcuts**:

o   You can also assign system-wide shortcuts (such as opening Mission Control with **F3** or locking your screen with **Control + Command + Q**).

5. **Test Your Shortcuts**:

o   Once created, use the keyboard shortcuts in the designated applications to boost your productivity.

Advanced Terminal Commands for Power Users:

The **Terminal** app is for advanced users who want to access and control macOS via text commands. You can use it to tweak system settings and perform powerful tasks.

1. **Open Terminal**:

   o Press **Command + Space**, type **Terminal**, and hit **Enter** to open it.

2. **Basic Commands**:

   o For beginners, start with basic commands like:

     ▪ **pwd**: Prints the current directory you are in.

     ▪ **ls**: Lists all files and directories in your current directory.

     ▪ **cd [folder name]**: Changes your current directory to the specified folder.

     ▪ **rm [file name]**: Deletes a file (use with caution).

3. **Advanced Customizations**:

   o You can use **Terminal** to adjust system behavior:

     ▪ **defaults write**: Allows you to change system settings, like speeding up the Finder window animation:

     `arduino`

```
defaults write com.apple.finder
AnimateWindowZoom    -bool
false killall Finder
```

- **sudo**: Use with caution as it grants admin-level access to your system. It's typically used for installing software or modifying system files.

AI and Machine Learning Features

The M4 chip brings powerful AI capabilities to the MacBook Air, enhancing various aspects of the device's performance, from processing tasks to optimizing apps.

How the M4 Chip Uses AI to Enhance Performance:

The M4 chip contains a **16-core Neural Engine** that processes tasks using machine learning. Here's how it benefits you:

1. **Faster Task Processing**:

    o The Neural Engine accelerates tasks that involve recognizing patterns or making predictions. This is particularly useful for:

        - **Photo and Video Editing**: AI can improve your editing process by automatically enhancing images and videos.

- **Speech Recognition**: Tools like **Siri** or dictation services become faster and more accurate.

- **Photo Management**: **Photos** app uses machine learning to automatically sort and categorize images based on content (e.g., faces, locations, objects).

2. **Optimized App Performance**:

   o Apps that use machine learning, such as **Photos**, **Mail**, and **Notes**, benefit from the M4's Neural Engine by becoming more responsive and efficient.

Machine Learning Apps and Their Benefits in Everyday Use:

1. **Photos App**:

   o AI automatically sorts images into albums by location, date, and even facial recognition.

   o It can suggest improvements for photos, such as adjusting exposure or highlighting details.

2. **Mail App**:

   o The M4 chip helps **Mail** filter spam emails more effectively by learning from patterns in your inbox.

- o **Mail** also uses AI to help prioritize important emails and automatically categorize them into focused inboxes.

3. **Photo Editing Apps (like Lightroom)**:

- o With AI-powered enhancements, Lightroom can suggest the best photo adjustments, saving time and effort for photographers.

Optimizing for Specific Tasks

Your MacBook Air is versatile enough to handle a variety of tasks, from gaming to creative work to software development. Here's how to optimize your MacBook for specific tasks.

Gaming on the MacBook Air (Casual Gaming Performance):

While the M4 chip offers solid graphics performance for casual gaming, keep in mind that the MacBook Air isn't designed for running demanding AAA games. However, it handles casual games well, such as **Stardew Valley** or **Minecraft**.

1. **Optimizing Game Settings**:

- o In **System Settings > Battery**, switch to **Low Power Mode** for gaming sessions to optimize battery life.

- o Adjust in-game settings to lower graphics quality for smoother performance.

2. **Use Game Streaming**:

- o Consider using game streaming services like **NVIDIA GeForce Now** or **Apple Arcade** for access to more demanding titles without relying on your MacBook's hardware.

3. **Connecting Game Controllers**:

   - o You can use Bluetooth controllers, like an Xbox or PlayStation controller, for a better gaming experience:

     - ▪ To connect, go to **System Settings > Bluetooth**, and pair your controller by pressing its Bluetooth pairing button.

Creative Work (Photo Editing, Video Editing, Music Production):

With the M4 chip, your MacBook Air can easily handle creative tasks like photo editing, music production, and video editing. Here's how to optimize it:

1. **Use AI-Powered Features in Creative Apps**:

   - o In **Photoshop** and **Lightroom**, use the AI-based tools to speed up tasks like selecting objects or adjusting lighting.

   - o In **Final Cut Pro**, AI features will help optimize your video rendering for faster processing times.

2. **Music Production**:

   - o Apps like **GarageBand** and **Logic Pro** are optimized for macOS. With the M4 chip, you can create and edit high-quality music with little lag.

Software Development with macOS (Setting Up for Coding):

macOS is a great environment for software development. With the power of the M4 chip, coding, compiling, and testing apps are smoother than ever.

1. **Install Xcode**:

   ○ Download and install **Xcode** from the **Mac App Store** for a comprehensive coding environment. This includes compilers, libraries, and simulators.

   ○ Once installed, open Xcode and start a new project to begin developing apps or software.

2. **Use Homebrew for Package Management**:

   ○ Open **Terminal**, and type the following to install **Homebrew** (a package manager for macOS):

   `bash`

   ```
   /bin/bash -c "$(curl -fsSL
   https://raw.githubusercontent.com/Hom
   ebrew/install/HEAD/install.sh)"
   ```

   ○ Use Homebrew to install tools like **Git**, **Node.js**, and more.

External Devices and Gaming Accessories

To further enhance your gaming and productivity experience, you can use various external devices and accessories.

Using External GPUs for Enhanced Graphics (if needed):

1. **Connect an External GPU (eGPU):**

   o The MacBook Air supports external GPUs via Thunderbolt 3 or USB-C, which can help boost performance for graphics-heavy tasks or gaming.

   o Purchase an **eGPU enclosure** with an appropriate graphics card (such as an **AMD Radeon** card) and connect it via a Thunderbolt 3 port.

2. **Use eGPU for Gaming:**

   o After connecting the eGPU, use macOS settings to direct graphic-heavy games to the external GPU for better performance.

Connecting Game Controllers for PC Games and Streaming:

1. **Pair Bluetooth Game Controllers:**

   o Open **System Settings > Bluetooth** and make sure Bluetooth is enabled.

o Put your game controller into pairing mode and select it when it appears in the Bluetooth menu.

With these advanced features and tips, you're now equipped to automate tasks, enhance productivity with AI, enjoy casual gaming, and optimize your MacBook Air for creative and coding projects. Keep experimenting with the tools available in macOS, and you'll find new ways to customize and personalize your experience to suit your needs.

BUSINESS USE AND ENTERPRISE INTEGRATION

This section is designed to guide you through using your MacBook Air for business tasks, integrating it into a corporate environment, and setting up business tools like email, VPNs, and enterprise solutions. Whether you're working from home, in an office, or on the go, this detailed guide will help you set up your MacBook for productivity and security.

MacBook Air for Business Professionals

The **MacBook Air** is a powerful yet portable device, ideal for business professionals who need to work efficiently on the go. Its lightweight design and long battery life make it perfect for remote work or daily office tasks.

Why the MacBook Air is Perfect for Remote Work and Business Tasks:

1. **Lightweight and Portable**:

    o **Step 1**: The MacBook Air is known for being incredibly lightweight (just 2.8 pounds). This makes it easy to carry around if you're frequently traveling for business or working remotely.

    o **Step 2**: It's also slim, with a 13.3-inch Retina display, providing a balance of screen real estate without taking up too much space in your bag.

2. **Long Battery Life**:

   o **Step 1**: With up to **18 hours of battery life**, the MacBook Air can easily get you through a full workday without needing a recharge.

   o **Step 2**: This is especially useful for remote work, as you can work for long hours at cafes, co-working spaces, or during travel without being tied to an outlet.

3. **macOS for Business Productivity**:

   o **Step 1**: The MacBook Air runs **macOS**, which supports a wide range of professional software for business tasks like **Microsoft Office** (Word, Excel, PowerPoint), **Google Workspace** (Docs, Sheets, Gmail), and **Slack** for team communication.

   o **Step 2**: Use **macOS Preview** to view and annotate PDF documents, and **macOS Notes** to jot down ideas or take meeting notes. Both are built into the system and easy to access.

4. **Seamless Collaboration**:

   o **Step 1**: If you're working with a team, use **iCloud Drive** to sync your documents across all Apple devices. This allows you to access and share business files from anywhere.

- o **Step 2**: You can also integrate **Google Drive** or **Dropbox** into macOS for cloud storage and collaborative work, so your team can access shared files in real-time.

5. **Communication Tools**:

- o **Step 1**: Use **Mail** for email communication and **Messages** for quick text-based communication with colleagues. Both apps are integrated seamlessly into macOS.

- o **Step 2**: The **FaceTime** app allows you to make video and audio calls to other Apple users, or you can install third-party apps like **Zoom** or **Microsoft Teams** for business meetings.

How to Set Up macOS for Project Management and Collaboration:

1. **Install Project Management Software**:

- o **Step 1**: If your team uses tools like **Trello**, **Asana**, or **Monday.com**, go to the **Mac App Store** and download the relevant apps, or use their web versions through Safari.

- o **Step 2**: Log into your project management account, sync your tasks, and begin organizing your work.

2. **Set Up Shared Folders**:

- o **Step 1**: Use **iCloud Drive** for seamless file syncing across devices. In **Finder**, drag and drop documents into iCloud Drive, and they'll automatically sync with all your Apple devices.

- o **Step 2**: For business teams using **Dropbox** or **Google Drive**, download and install their desktop apps from their respective websites. These allow you to keep important documents accessible and synced across devices.

3. **Enable Calendar and Reminders**:

    - o **Step 1**: Set up **macOS Calendar** with your work-related meetings, deadlines, and events. You can sync it with **Google Calendar**, **Outlook**, or **Exchange** for unified scheduling.

    - o **Step 2**: Use **Reminders** to track your to-do list and assign tasks, keeping you organized and on top of your business tasks.

Business Security and VPNs

For remote work or business transactions, security is paramount. Setting up a **VPN** and using built-in **FileVault** encryption are key steps in ensuring your work data remains secure.

Setting Up a Virtual Private Network (VPN) on macOS:

A **VPN (Virtual Private Network)** allows you to securely connect to a remote server, encrypting your internet connection and ensuring that your online activities remain private.

1. **Choose a VPN Provider**:

    o **Step 1**: Sign up for a reliable VPN service like **NordVPN**, **ExpressVPN**, or **CyberGhost**. Many businesses provide VPN accounts to employees for secure access to company resources.

    o **Step 2**: Once you've signed up, you'll usually be given installation instructions from the VPN provider.

2. **Install the VPN Application**:

    o **Step 1**: Most VPN providers have their own macOS apps. Download and install the app from the **Mac App Store** or directly from the VPN provider's website.

    o **Step 2**: Once installed, open the VPN app and log in with your account details.

3. **Configure the VPN on macOS**:

    o **Step 1**: Open **System Settings** (Apple logo > **System Settings**).

    o **Step 2**: Click **Network**, and then **Add a VPN Connection**. Choose **VPN** as the interface type.

- Step 3: Enter the necessary server information provided by your VPN service, and click **Connect**.

4. **Test the VPN Connection**:
   - Step 1: After setting up the VPN, you'll see a **VPN icon** at the top of your screen, indicating that the connection is active.
   - Step 2: You can now securely browse the internet or access business resources remotely, knowing that your connection is encrypted.

Enabling Encryption with FileVault for Security:

FileVault is macOS's built-in disk encryption tool, which encrypts all the files on your hard drive to prevent unauthorized access.

1. **Turn on FileVault**:
   - Step 1: Go to **System Settings > Privacy & Security**.
   - Step 2: Under the **FileVault** section, click **Turn On FileVault**.
   - Step 3: Follow the on-screen instructions to set up a recovery key, which will allow you to unlock your Mac if you forget your password.

2. **Complete the Setup**:
   - Step 1: FileVault will now begin encrypting the files on your MacBook

Air. This may take some time, depending on the amount of data you have stored.

- o **Step 2**: Once the process is complete, all your data will be encrypted, offering an extra layer of security.

Enterprise Integration

Integrating your MacBook Air into a business environment can involve using enterprise tools like **Microsoft Teams, Slack, Zoom**, and managing devices through **Apple Business Manager**. Here's how to make these tools work for you:

Integrating with Microsoft Teams, Slack, and Zoom:

1. **Microsoft Teams**:

   - o **Step 1**: Download **Microsoft Teams** from the **Mac App Store** or the official Microsoft website.

   - o **Step 2**: Open Teams, sign in with your work or school account, and access channels for team communication and file sharing.

   - o **Step 3**: You can also schedule and join video meetings within the app.

2. **Slack**:

   - o **Step 1**: Download **Slack** from the **Mac App Store** or their website.

   - o **Step 2**: Log in with your business Slack workspace credentials.

- o **Step 3**: Create channels, send direct messages, share files, and collaborate with your team in real-time.

3. **Zoom**:

  - o **Step 1**: Install **Zoom** from the **Mac App Store** or directly from the Zoom website.

  - o **Step 2**: Open Zoom, sign in with your Zoom account, and schedule or join video meetings.

  - o **Step 3**: You can share screens, use chat, and conduct video meetings for remote work and collaboration.

Managing Devices with Apple Business Manager:

Apple Business Manager (ABM) helps companies set up and manage MacBook Air devices for employees.

1. **Setting Up ABM**:

  - o **Step 1**: Your company's IT administrator must sign up for **Apple Business Manager**. This service is designed to help businesses deploy and manage Apple devices in bulk.

  - o **Step 2**: IT administrators can create accounts for employees and assign devices to them directly from the ABM portal.

2. **Device Enrollment**:

o **Step 1**: Once enrolled in ABM, you'll receive a **Company Apple ID** that can be used to configure your MacBook Air with corporate settings.

o **Step 2**: IT administrators can remotely configure your MacBook, install necessary business apps, and set up security policies.

Using macOS with Active Directory in Business Environments:

Many businesses use **Active Directory (AD)** to manage user accounts and access to resources. Here's how to integrate macOS with Active Directory:

1. **Join Your MacBook to Active Directory**:

    o **Step 1**: Open **System Settings** and go to **Users & Groups**.

    o **Step 2**: Click **Login Options**, and then click **Join** next to **Network Account Server**.

    o **Step 3**: Enter the domain details for your company's Active Directory server.

2. **Access Corporate Resources**:

    o **Step 1**: After joining the domain, you'll be able to log into your MacBook using your **Active Directory** credentials.

    o **Step 2**: You can access network drives, shared resources, and corporate email through the company's directory.

With these easy-to-follow instructions, you'll be able to fully harness the power of your MacBook Air for all your business needs. Whether you're setting up a secure remote workspace, using key enterprise tools, or integrating with your company's systems, you'll have everything you need to stay productive and secure. Your MacBook Air will quickly become an essential tool for getting work done efficiently and safely, no matter where you are.

GAMING AND ENTERTAINMENT

Your MacBook Air is designed to handle a variety of tasks, from productivity to entertainment. In this section, we'll cover how to get the most out of your MacBook Air for gaming and entertainment, including tips on gaming performance, game streaming services, and the best ways to enjoy media.

Gaming on the MacBook Air

Performance Expectations for Gaming (Casual vs. Intensive Games)

The MacBook Air is equipped with the powerful M4 chip, making it more than capable of handling casual games and lighter titles. However, it's important to manage your expectations when it comes to more intensive gaming (like AAA titles). Here's what you can expect based on the type of game:

- **Casual Games (Low to Medium Demands)**: The MacBook Air performs excellently for casual games like *Minecraft*, *Stardew Valley*, *The Sims*, and other less graphically demanding games. These types of games should run smoothly at medium to high settings.

- **Intensive Games (High Demands)**: The MacBook Air can struggle with graphically demanding games like *Red Dead Redemption 2* or *Cyberpunk 2077* due to its integrated graphics. These games are better suited for higher-end Macs with discrete GPUs or gaming PCs.

104

However, you can still play these games at lower settings, but be prepared for some performance limitations.

- **Ideal Settings for Gaming**: To ensure optimal gaming performance, lower your game settings if you notice lag. Reducing graphic-intensive features (like shadow effects, textures, or anti-aliasing) can help smooth out gameplay.

Recommended Games for MacBook Air Users

If you're a casual gamer or just looking for a fun way to unwind, here are some games that run well on the MacBook Air:

- **Stardew Valley** – A farming simulation game that is light on system resources, yet fun and engaging.

- **Civilization VI** – A strategy game that runs well on macOS, perfect for gamers who love to build empires and make strategic decisions.

- **SimCity BuildIt** – A city-building game that requires little hardware power, but provides hours of entertainment.

- **Fortnite (Low settings)** – A popular battle royale game that can be played on lower settings for good performance.

These games will provide smooth experiences while you enjoy gaming on the go.

Game Streaming: Using GeForce Now, Steam Link, and Cloud Gaming Services

For more graphically demanding games, you can take advantage of **game streaming services**. These services allow you to stream games from the cloud, so you don't need a powerful machine to enjoy the latest titles. Here's how to use them:

1. **GeForce Now**:

    o **What it is**: GeForce Now allows you to stream PC games on your MacBook Air. It connects you to high-performance gaming PCs in the cloud.

    o **How to use it**:

        1. **Download and Install**: Visit the GeForce Now website and download the app.

        2. **Sign Up**: Create an account or log in with an existing one.

        3. **Link Your Game Library**: Connect your Steam, Epic Games, or Uplay account to access your library.

        4. **Start Playing**: Choose a game from your library and start streaming. Ensure you have a fast, stable internet connection (preferably 15 Mbps or higher) for smooth streaming.

2. **Steam Link**:

    o **What it is**: Steam Link allows you to stream games from your gaming PC to your MacBook Air. You'll need to have a gaming PC with Steam installed.

- o **How to use it**:

    1. **Download the Steam Link app** from the Mac App Store.

    2. **Connect to Your PC**: Ensure your gaming PC and MacBook Air are on the same Wi-Fi network.

    3. **Stream and Play**: Open Steam on your gaming PC, then launch the Steam Link app on your MacBook. Follow the on-screen instructions to pair both devices and start playing.

3. **Cloud Gaming Services** (Xbox Cloud Gaming, PlayStation Now):

    - o **What it is**: These services let you play console games on your MacBook Air by streaming directly from the cloud.

    - o **How to use it**:

        1. **Sign Up** for services like Xbox Cloud Gaming (available through Xbox Game Pass Ultimate) or PlayStation Now.

        2. **Access Through Browser or App**: For Xbox Cloud Gaming, you can access it through a browser (Edge or Chrome

recommended). For PlayStation Now, you'll need to download the PlayStation Now app for macOS.

3. **Start Gaming**: Once set up, select a game from the library and start streaming.

Entertainment on macOS

The MacBook Air is also perfect for enjoying movies, TV shows, music, and more. Let's dive into how you can enhance your entertainment experience with macOS.

Streaming Movies and TV Shows (Apple TV+, Netflix, Disney+)

Streaming content is one of the MacBook Air's strong points, thanks to its beautiful Retina display and great audio system. Here's how to get started:

1. **Apple TV+**:

   o **What it is**: Apple TV+ is Apple's exclusive streaming service offering a variety of original shows and movies.

   o **How to use it**:

      1. **Download the Apple TV App** from the Mac App Store if it's not pre-installed.

      2. **Sign In** with your Apple ID to access your Apple TV+ subscription.

3. **Browse Content**: Use the search feature or explore curated sections to find the latest Apple TV+ content.

4. **Start Streaming**: Click on a show or movie to start watching.

2. **Netflix**:

   o **What it is**: Netflix is a popular streaming service with a huge library of movies, TV shows, and documentaries.

   o **How to use it**:

      1. **Go to the Netflix Website**: Open Safari or your preferred browser and go to www.netflix.com.

      2. **Sign In**: Use your Netflix account details to sign in.

      3. **Browse**: Use categories or the search bar to find something to watch.

      4. **Start Watching**: Click on a title to start streaming.

3. **Disney+**:

   o **What it is**: Disney+ offers a vast collection of Disney movies, Pixar films, Marvel TV shows and movies, Star Wars content, and National Geographic.

- How to use it:

  1. **Sign Up for Disney+**: Go to www.disneyplus.com and create an account if you don't have one already.

  2. **Sign In**: Log in with your credentials.

  3. **Browse and Select**: Navigate through the categories to find the content you love, and start streaming.

Using Apple Music and Spotify for Music Streaming

For music lovers, the MacBook Air is perfect for enjoying music through platforms like Apple Music and Spotify.

1. **Apple Music**:

   - **What it is**: Apple Music is Apple's music streaming service with a vast library of songs, playlists, and exclusive content.

   - **How to use it**:

     1. **Open the Music App** on your MacBook Air (pre-installed with macOS).

     2. **Sign In**: Log in using your Apple ID if you have an Apple Music subscription.

3. **Browse**: Explore curated playlists, albums, and songs or search for specific tracks.

4. **Create Playlists**: Click the plus (+) button next to songs to create custom playlists.

5. **Start Listening**: Hit play to enjoy your favorite music.

2. **Spotify**:

   o **What it is**: Spotify is one of the most popular music streaming platforms, with millions of songs and playlists.

   o **How to use it**:

      1. **Download the Spotify App**: You can download it from the Mac App Store or visit the Spotify website to access the web player.

      2. **Sign In**: Log in with your existing Spotify account.

      3. **Browse or Search**: Look through your favorite artists, albums, or playlists.

      4. **Listen**: Select any song, album, or playlist to start playing your music.

Setting Up Plex or Jellyfin for Media Servers

If you have a collection of media (movies, TV shows, music, etc.) stored on your MacBook Air or external drives, you can set up a **media server** to access and stream your media across devices.

1. **Plex**:

    o **What it is**: Plex is a popular media server software that organizes your media and allows you to stream it on any device.

    o **How to use it**:

        1. **Download Plex**: Visit the Plex website and create an account.

        2. **Install Plex Media Server** on your MacBook Air.

        3. **Add Media**: Add your media files (movies, TV shows, music) to your Plex library.

        4. **Stream Content**: Install the Plex app on any device (iPhone, smart TV, etc.) to stream your media.

2. **Jellyfin**:

    o **What it is**: Jellyfin is an open-source alternative to Plex that allows you to organize and stream media.

    o **How to use it**:

        1. **Download Jellyfin**: Go to the Jellyfin website and install the

server software on your MacBook Air.

2. **Configure Your Library**: Add your media to the Jellyfin library.

3. **Access from Any Device**: Use the Jellyfin app or web player on your other devices to stream your content.

Your MacBook Air is an excellent device for both gaming and entertainment, offering powerful features for both light gaming and media consumption. Whether you're gaming casually, streaming movies and TV shows, or enjoying your favorite music, you can easily tailor your MacBook Air to meet all your entertainment needs!

TROUBLESHOOTING AND SUPPORT

Even though the MacBook Air is designed to be intuitive and reliable, problems can sometimes occur. This section will guide you through common troubleshooting steps to resolve issues, and show you how to access Apple Support and warranty services if necessary.

Common Problems and Solutions

MacBook Air Won't Turn On: Steps to Fix It

If your MacBook Air is unresponsive and won't turn on, there could be several reasons behind it. Here's how to troubleshoot the issue:

Step 1: Check Power and Charging

1. **Ensure the MacBook Air is Charged**: Plug your MacBook Air into a power source using the provided charger. Check if the charging indicator light on the adapter (if available) is on.

2. **Wait for a Few Minutes**: Sometimes, if the battery is completely drained, it may take a few minutes before the MacBook Air shows signs of life.

3. **Inspect the Charging Cable**: Check if the charging cable is damaged. If you have another charger that's compatible, try using it to see if that resolves the issue.

Step 2: Perform a Hard Reset

1. **Press and Hold the Power Button**: Press and hold the power button for 10 seconds to force a hard reset. Then, release the button and press it again to see if the MacBook starts up.

2. **Reset the SMC (System Management Controller)**: The SMC controls many hardware functions. Resetting it can often resolve power issues:

   - **For M1 or M2 Macs**: Shut down the MacBook. Press and hold the power button for 10 seconds, then release. Wait a few seconds and turn the MacBook on again.

   - **For Intel-based Macs**: Shut down the MacBook, then press and hold the left Shift + Control + Option keys and the power button at the same time for 10 seconds. Release the keys, wait a few seconds, and turn the MacBook on.

Step 3: Try Safe Mode

1. **Boot into Safe Mode**: Turn on your Mac and immediately press and hold the **Shift key**. Keep holding until you see the login window. Safe Mode will perform a basic check of your system and attempt to repair any issues preventing startup.

2. If you can boot into Safe Mode, try restarting the Mac normally to see if the issue persists.

Fixing Wi-Fi Issues and Slow Internet Connections

Wi-Fi connectivity problems can be frustrating, but there are several steps you can take to troubleshoot and resolve them.

Step 1: Check Wi-Fi Connection

1. **Ensure Wi-Fi Is On**: Click on the Wi-Fi icon in the top-right corner of your screen and make sure Wi-Fi is turned on. If it's turned off, click the icon and turn it back on.

2. **Check Your Router**: If you're having trouble connecting to your network, check if the issue is with your Wi-Fi router. Ensure that it is powered on and functioning correctly. Try restarting your router by unplugging it for 10 seconds, then plugging it back in.

Step 2: Forget and Reconnect to Wi-Fi Network

1. **Forget Network**: Go to **System Preferences > Network > Wi-Fi > Advanced**. Select the network you are having trouble with and click the **minus (-)** button to remove it.

2. **Reconnect**: After forgetting the network, reconnect by clicking the Wi-Fi icon, selecting the network, and entering the password.

Step 3: Run Wireless Diagnostics

1. Hold down the **Option key** and click the Wi-Fi icon in the top-right corner of your screen.

2. Select **Open Wireless Diagnostics** from the dropdown.

3. Follow the on-screen instructions to diagnose and resolve issues.

Step 4: Restart Your MacBook

1. Simply restarting your Mac can often resolve many issues. To do this, click the Apple logo in the top-left corner of the screen, then select **Restart**.

Step 5: Reset the Network Settings

1. If the issue persists, go to **System Preferences > Network > Wi-Fi**, and click the **Advanced** button. In the "Preferred Networks" list, click the **minus (-)** button to remove any old, problematic networks. Then, reconnect to your current network.

MacBook Not Charging: Troubleshooting and Solutions

If your MacBook Air isn't charging, follow these steps to resolve the issue:

Step 1: Check the Charging Cable and Adapter

1. **Inspect the Charging Cable and Adapter**: Ensure there are no visible signs of damage to the charging cable or adapter. If you have another compatible charger, try using it to see if your MacBook charges.

Step 2: Check the Charging Port

1. **Clean the Charging Port**: Sometimes dust or debris can accumulate in the charging port, preventing the charger from making a proper

connection. Use a dry, soft brush or compressed air to clean the port.

Step 3: Reset the SMC (System Management Controller)

1. For M1 and M2 Macs: Shut down the Mac, press and hold the power button for 10 seconds, and then turn the Mac back on.

2. For Intel-based Macs: Shut down the Mac, press and hold the left Shift + Control + Option keys and the power button at the same time for 10 seconds. Release the keys, wait a few seconds, and turn the MacBook on.

Step 4: Check Battery Health

1. **Check Battery Health**: To see if your battery is healthy, click the **Apple logo** in the top-left corner, then choose **About This Mac > System Report > Power**. Here you can check the battery's condition. If it reads "Service Battery," it may need to be replaced.

Apple Support and Warranty

If you've tried the troubleshooting steps and the issue persists, it might be time to contact Apple Support or visit an Apple Store. Here's how to get help:

Step 1: Using AppleCare and Apple Support

1. **AppleCare+**: Apple offers AppleCare+ which extends your warranty coverage and provides tech support. If you have AppleCare+ or your warranty is still valid, you can contact Apple

Support for repairs, replacements, and technical assistance.

2. **Contact Apple Support**: To contact Apple Support, visit the Apple Support website or use the **Apple Support app** (available on the Mac App Store). You can either chat with a representative or schedule a phone call.

Step 2: Visit an Apple Store or Authorized Service Provider

1. **Find a Nearby Apple Store**: Visit the Apple Store locator to find the closest store. You can also schedule a Genius Bar appointment through the Apple Support website or app.

2. **Authorized Service Providers**: If you don't have an Apple Store nearby, you can also visit an Apple Authorized Service Provider for repairs.

Step 3: What to Do if Your MacBook Air Needs Repairs

1. If you need repairs, be prepared with your MacBook Air's **serial number** (found in **System Preferences > About This Mac**), and a brief description of the problem.

2. Apple Support will provide the necessary instructions for repairs, which may include shipping your MacBook Air to Apple or visiting a local service center.

Tips for Keeping Your MacBook Air Running Smoothly

Taking care of your MacBook Air is essential to keep it performing at its best. Here are some tips for maintaining your MacBook:

Best Practices for Preventing Software and Hardware Issues

1. **Keep Software Up to Date**: Ensure that macOS and all apps are updated to their latest versions. Apple regularly releases updates that fix bugs and improve system performance.

   o To check for updates, go to **Apple Menu > System Preferences > Software Update**.

2. **Regularly Restart Your Mac**: Restart your Mac at least once a week to keep the system running smoothly. This helps refresh the system and clear out temporary files that can slow down performance.

3. **Avoid Overloading the System**: Don't keep too many apps or browser tabs open at the same time. Close unnecessary apps to avoid slowing down the system.

4. **Use Disk Utility for Maintenance**: Regularly check your Mac's hard drive for errors.

   o To do this, open **Disk Utility** (found in **Applications > Utilities**), select your startup disk, and click **First Aid** to check for and repair disk issues.

Keeping macOS Updated and Secured

1. **Update macOS Regularly**: Always install the latest macOS updates as they include security patches and bug fixes.

   o **Automatic Updates**: Go to **System Preferences** > **Software Update**, and check the box for **Automatically keep my Mac up to date**.

2. **Set Up Time Machine Backups**: Regular backups ensure you don't lose any important data in case of hardware failure. Set up **Time Machine** to back up your system to an external drive or network drive.

   o Go to **System Preferences** > **Time Machine**, and select a backup disk to start the backup process.

By following these steps and tips, you can keep your MacBook Air running smoothly and avoid most common issues. If you encounter any problems that can't be fixed on your own, Apple Support is there to help you every step of the way!

QUICK TIPS AND TRICKS

If you want to get the most out of your MacBook Air, there are many hidden features, shortcuts, and fun tricks that can make your experience smoother and more enjoyable. Here, we'll walk you through some essential keyboard shortcuts that can improve your productivity and also show you some fun things you can try with your MacBook Air to add a little bit of personality and fun to your device.

Essential macOS Keyboard Shortcuts

Using keyboard shortcuts is a great way to navigate macOS more efficiently, saving time and making your work faster. Below are some of the most useful and essential keyboard shortcuts you should know:

Boosting Productivity with Keyboard Shortcuts

1. **Command + C (Copy) and Command + V (Paste)**

   o **What it does**: Copies and pastes selected text, files, or items.

   o **How to use it**: Highlight the text or file you want to copy, press **Command + C** to copy it, navigate to where you want to paste it, and press **Command + V**.

2. **Command + X (Cut)**

- o **What it does**: Cuts selected text or items to be moved elsewhere.

- o **How to use it**: Highlight what you want to cut, press **Command + X** to remove it, and then **Command + V** to paste it in a new location.

3. **Command + Z (Undo)**

- o **What it does**: Undoes the last action you performed.

- o **How to use it**: Press **Command + Z** if you make a mistake and want to undo your last action.

4. **Command + Shift + 4 (Screenshot)**

- o **What it does**: Takes a screenshot of a selected area on your screen.

- o **How to use it**: Press **Command + Shift + 4**. The cursor will change to a crosshair. Click and drag to select the area you want to capture, and it will save automatically to your desktop.

5. **Command + Space (Spotlight Search)**

- o **What it does**: Opens Spotlight Search, allowing you to quickly find files, apps, emails, or even search the web.

- o **How to use it**: Press **Command + Space**, type what you're looking for, and Spotlight will show you results instantly.

This is a super fast way to find anything on your Mac.

6. **Command + Tab (Switch Between Apps)**

   o **What it does**: Allows you to quickly cycle between open apps.

   o **How to use it**: Hold **Command** and tap **Tab** to switch between open applications. This helps you quickly toggle between tasks without needing to use the mouse.

7. **Command + W (Close Window)**

   o **What it does**: Closes the active window.

   o **How to use it**: When you're done with a window, just press **Command + W** to close it without having to click the "X" button.

8. **Command + Q (Quit App)**

   o **What it does**: Quits the current application completely.

   o **How to use it**: Press **Command + Q** to quit the current app, ensuring it's fully closed. This can help with performance if you have many apps running in the background.

Hidden macOS Tips for Faster Navigation

1. **Mission Control (F3)**

o **What it does**: Shows all open windows in a bird's eye view.

o **How to use it**: Press the **F3 key** (or swipe up with three fingers on your trackpad). This will give you an overview of all your open windows, helping you navigate between them easily. You can also drag windows between desktops if you're using multiple workspaces.

2. **Command + H (Hide Window)**

o **What it does**: Hides the current app window without closing it.

o **How to use it**: Press **Command + H** to quickly hide the current window. You can access it again from the Dock or by clicking the app's icon in the top-left corner of the screen.

3. **Command + Shift + T (Reopen Closed Tabs)**

o **What it does**: Reopens the last closed tab in your browser.

o **How to use it**: If you accidentally close a tab in Safari, Chrome, or another browser, simply press **Command + Shift + T** to reopen it.

4. **Option + Command + Esc (Force Quit)**

o **What it does**: Opens the Force Quit window to close unresponsive apps.

- o **How to use it**: Press **Option + Command + Esc** to bring up the **Force Quit Applications** window, where you can select and close any app that isn't responding.

5. **Trackpad Gestures**

   - o **What it does**: Enables multiple ways to interact with macOS using the trackpad.

   - o **How to use it**:

     - **Swipe up with three fingers**: Opens Mission Control.

     - **Swipe left or right with three fingers**: Switch between full-screen apps or desktops.

     - **Pinch with three fingers**: Zoom in or out on a webpage or document.

Fun Things to Try with Your MacBook Air

Your MacBook Air isn't just for work—it's also packed with fun features that you can use to personalize your experience and try new activities. Let's take a look at some fun things you can do with your MacBook Air!

Using Siri for Voice Commands and Fun Tasks

Siri is Apple's virtual assistant that can help with a variety of tasks, from setting reminders to playing music and even telling jokes. Here's how to use Siri for fun and productivity:

Step 1: Enable Siri

1. Go to **Apple Menu > System Preferences > Siri**.

2. Make sure Siri is turned on by checking the box that says **Enable Ask Siri**.

3. You can also choose to use **"Hey Siri"** for hands-free commands.

Step 2: Ask Siri Fun Questions or Give Commands

1. To activate Siri, say **"Hey Siri"** or press and hold the **Command + Spacebar**.

2. Ask Siri fun questions like:

   o   "Hey Siri, tell me a joke!"

   o   "Hey Siri, what's the weather today?"

   o   "Hey Siri, what's the meaning of life?"

3. You can also use Siri to perform useful tasks:

   o   "Hey Siri, set a reminder for 3 PM."

   o   "Hey Siri, open Safari."

   o   "Hey Siri, play music by [artist]."

Customizing Your Mac with Fun Themes and Widgets

Make your MacBook Air more personalized by adding themes, widgets, and changing its appearance:

Step 1: Change Your Desktop Wallpaper

1. **Right-click** on the desktop and choose **Change Desktop Background**.

2. You can choose from the default Apple wallpapers, or click the + button to select a custom image from your photos or a downloaded image.

Step 2: Add Widgets to the Notification Center

1. **Open the Notification Center** by clicking the icon in the top-right corner of your screen.

2. Scroll down and click **Edit Widgets**.

3. From here, you can add widgets like the weather, calendar, or notes to quickly access important information without opening an app.

Step 3: Set Live Wallpapers

1. Download live wallpapers from third-party websites or use apps like **Wallpaper Wizard 2** or **Desktop Live Wallpapers**.

2. After downloading, set the live wallpaper the same way you would a regular wallpaper by going to **System Preferences > Desktop & Screen Saver**.

By using these keyboard shortcuts and fun activities, you can become a more efficient MacBook Air user while also making your device more personal and enjoyable. Experiment with different features, and soon you'll be navigating macOS like a pro, all while having fun along the way!

CONCLUSION

Congratulations! You've now been guided through every essential aspect of your MacBook Air, from setup to advanced features, and troubleshooting. By exploring its key features, including productivity tools, customization options, security settings, and more, you are well on your way to mastering your MacBook Air and making the most of its capabilities.

The MacBook Air is a powerful device that can be tailored to meet your personal needs, whether you're using it for work, entertainment, creativity, or productivity. Remember, it's not just about using your MacBook—it's about making it yours. Customize your system settings, explore new applications, and integrate it into your life in ways that enhance your workflow and enjoyment.

Resources for Ongoing Learning

The journey with your MacBook Air doesn't end here. There's always more to learn! Here are a few tips to keep growing with your Mac:

1. **Explore the Apple Support Website**: The official Apple support site has in-depth articles, troubleshooting guides, and step-by-step tutorials. It's a great resource when you need more specific help or want to discover new features.

2. **Join Mac Communities**: Online forums and communities like MacRumors, Reddit's MacBook section, and Apple's own community are great places to learn new tips, ask questions,

and stay up-to-date on the latest MacBook Air news.

3. **Learn with Video Tutorials**: Websites like YouTube and online learning platforms offer countless tutorials on how to use macOS and the MacBook Air to its fullest. Whether you want to master a specific app or learn how to take better advantage of macOS, there are many videos that can help.

4. **Check for macOS Updates**: Apple regularly updates macOS, adding new features and enhancing existing ones. Be sure to keep your MacBook Air up to date by enabling **Automatic Updates** in **System Preferences > Software Update**.

5. **Experiment and Practice**: The best way to learn is by doing. Keep exploring, playing around with new apps, and experimenting with system preferences. Over time, you'll become more efficient and comfortable with your MacBook Air.

Now that you have all the tools and information to set up, personalize, and optimize your MacBook Air, it's time to get creative! Set up your workflow, install the apps you need, explore macOS features like automation and productivity tools, and start using your MacBook Air for everything it has to offer. Whether it's for personal, work, or creative use, your MacBook Air is ready to support you in all your endeavors.

The more you explore and customize your MacBook Air, the more it will become an indispensable part of your life.

So, take your time, dive into the world of macOS, and make your MacBook Air work for you in the best way possible.

Here's to your journey with your new MacBook Air— enjoy it to the fullest!

www.ingramcontent.com/pod-product-compliance
Lightning Source LLC
LaVergne TN
LVHW022350060326
832902LV00022B/4364